THE LITTLE BOOK OF
FORMULA 1

First published in Great Britain in 2026 by Cassell, an imprint of
Octopus Publishing Group Ltd
Carmelite House
50 Victoria Embankment
London EC4Y 0DZ
www.octopusbooks.co.uk

An Hachette UK Company
www.hachette.co.uk

The authorized representative in the EEA is
Hachette Ireland
8 Castlecourt Centre, Dublin 15, D15 XTP3
email: info@hbgi.ie

Distributed in the US by Hachette Book Group
1290 Avenue of the Americas, 4th and 5th Floors
New York, NY 10104

Distributed in Canada by Canadian Manda Group
664 Annette St., Toronto, Ontario, Canada
M6S 2C8

This book was conceived, designed, and produced by The Bright Press, an imprint of the Quarto Group,
1 Triptych Place, 185 Park Street,
London, United Kingdom, SE1 9SH
T (0)2077 009 000
www.Quarto.com

Publisher: James Evans
Editorial Director: Isheeta Mustafi
Managing Editor: Lucy Tipton
Art Director: Emily Nazer
Commissioning Editor: Caroline Elliker
Senior Editor: Joanna Bentley
Project Editor: Frank Hopkinson
Design: Cara Rogers

ISBN: 978-1-78840-699-4
eISBN: 978-1-78840-709-0

A CIP catalogue record for this book is available from the British Library.

Printed and bound in Guangdong, China.

TT/06/26

10 9 8 7 6 5 4 3 2 1

MIX
Paper | Supporting responsible forestry
FSC® C016973
FSC www.fsc.org

This FSC® label means that materials used for the product have been responsibly sourced.

THE LITTLE BOOK OF FORMULA 1

THE ILLUSTRATED GUIDE
TO AN ICONIC SPORT

FRANK HOPKINSON

CONTENTS

LAS VEGAS
QATAR AIRWAYS
DHL
DHL
DHL
QATAR AIRWAYS
QATAR AIRWAYS
WAYS

INTRODUCTION

If you took the 21 starters for the first Formula 1 grand prix at Silverstone in 1950 and put them on the grid 75 years later, alongside their modern-day counterparts, they might well think they had entered the realms of science fiction. F1 has been transformed from a sport of hobbyist, gentleman racers drifting their pre-war machinery around straw bales and oil drums to a global business with revenues of $4 billion. Today, should a car stop on track in an awkward place, it is covered by a Virtual Safety Car, in some cases a full Safety Car. In the 1970 Spanish Grand Prix at Jarama, Jackie Oliver collided with Jacky Ickx's Ferrari on the opening lap, sending both into the barriers with the cars erupting in flames. The drivers escaped with minor injuries but, laden with fuel, both cars burned furiously for an hour. The race continued regardless, with the remaining drivers having to steer a narrow path away from the wreckage, occasionally spinning on the foam and water that was now covering the circuit.

In the early 1950s a successful F1 team, such as Ferrari, might have 20 employees. Today, the Scuderia employs over a thousand. *The Little Book of F1* will take you on the journey that F1 has made through its epic history, from its earliest form to the global showstopper it has become.

LEFT: The start of the British Grand Prix in 2025, 75 years on from F1's first official race.

Denny Hulme
CHAMPION
GOOD YEAR
1
1

THE EVOLUTION OF F1

22
22

THE ROAD FROM SILVERSTONE

1950 TO 1961

International motor racing began in Europe at the turn of the 20th century with New York publisher, Gordon Bennett, sponsoring the Gordon Bennett Cup, a long-distance road race between national teams. Each chose their own national racing colour; France opted for Blue, Italy Red, Germany White, and Britain Shamrock Green. Those national colours would continue through to F1 and last until the late 1960s. The earliest races were from city to city, necessitating drivers to carry a riding mechanic – preferably not a heavy one.

The first official 'grand prix' which bucked the trend was held near Le Mans in 1906. The French Grand Prix was run over two days on a closed circuit of 103 km (64 miles), each day consisting of six laps. It was won by Hungarian Ferenc Zsisz driving a Renault. French marques dominated early continental racing with companies such as Richard-Brasier, Panhard and Delage. By the 1920s, Italian engineering was in the ascendancy, and some of the classic circuits were taking shape.

PREVIOUS PAGE: Denny Hulme and Bruce McLaren (r) waiting for practice to start at Jarama in 1968.
TOP LEFT: Giuseppe 'Nino' Farina was F1's first world champion, driving for Alfa Romeo.
LEFT: The third F1 race, held at Bremgarten, Switzerland. Alberto Ascari is far right, shaking hands.

Monza, Spa, the Nürburgring and Monaco all ran races in the 1920s, Bugatti triumphing in Monaco in 1929. By the 1930s the fascist regimes of Germany and Italy were investing huge sums in their national teams, with the Silver Arrows of Mercedes and Auto Union dominating the two Donington Grands Prix held in Britain.

Following the resumption of racing after WWII it was the Italian marques of Alfa Romeo, Maserati and Ferrari battling for honours, along with Talbot-Lago and Simca-Gordini of France. In 1950, the Commission Sportive Internationale (CSI) felt confident they had enough entrants for the first international championship. They had defined Formula 1, or Formula A, in 1946 based on engine capacity, with many countries running non-championship grand prix for spectators eager to see racing action. The lack of machinery often meant that lesser capacity Formula 2 cars made up the grid numbers.

Teams were financed by 'starting money' and prize money offered by the circuits, along with sponsorship from fuel, oil and tyre suppliers. Drivers were largely private individuals. Only the top teams could afford to employ professionals, such as Fangio, Farina, Ascari and Moss. The teams would also make extra income selling their cars to privateers. The archetypal car of the 1950s was the Maserati 250F, of which 26 were built between 1954 and 1957, far more than the factory team needed.

ABOVE: At Reims in 1959, the rear-engined Coopers were dwarfed by the Ferraris.

TOP: The 'garagistes' of Surbiton at Silverstone in 1960.
ABOVE LEFT: Roy Salvadori at the wheel of the Vanwall V4 in Rouen.
ABOVE RIGHT: Two 'sharknose' Ferrari 156s in the pits at the 1961 Belgian GP.

'Nino' Farina became the first drivers' champion in 1950 for Alfa Romeo, but it was not until 1958 that the constructors' title was introduced. It was won by the Vanwall team and marked the ascendancy of British race engineering. Jaguar had already won Le Mans five times and the Cooper Car Company, with its lightweight, rear-engined T43, had clinched its first F1 victory, the 1957 Argentine GP. The Cooper team, operating out of a small garage in Surbiton, would draw the ire of Enzo Ferrari in later years, describing his new rivals as 'garagistes'.

The Italian marque was late in switching to rear-engined cars and their first attempt in 1960, the Ferrari Dino 246, only achieved modest results. But its successor, the 156 'sharknose', was not only fast, it was beautiful. In the hands of Phil Hill and the likeable, aristocratic Wolfgang von Trips it dominated the 1961 championship. Von Trips was on the verge of winning the drivers' title at Monza when he hooked a wheel with Jim Clark in the opening laps. He was flung out of the car like a rag doll while the car barrel-rolled up the banking near Parabolica. The fear of being trapped in a burning vehicle was so strong that drivers preferred to take their chances and race without seat belts. Ferrari drivers Peter Collins and Luigi Musso had suffered similar fates in 1958, and the 1960s would only reinforce the verdict that being a Formula 1 driver was a perilous occupation.

YEARS OF LIVING DANGEROUSLY

1962-1982

In the 1960s and 1970s there was revolution in the air. Racing became more professional and the series better organized. While the boss of the Brabham team, Bernie Ecclestone, challenged the sport's governing body to hand over more of the TV revenue, the drivers organized themselves into the Grand Prix Drivers' Association and campaigned for safer circuits. The gung-ho spirit of surviving the war had been replaced by safety-conscious drivers who saw the frightening consequences of high-speed accidents.

Jackie Stewart was at the forefront for demanding more barriers at critical points of Spa and the Nürburgring, which he memorably dubbed 'The Green Hell'. Both classic tracks were boycotted and dropped from the calendar. Critics could hardly point to the Scot's inability to master the circuits. In 1968 he started sixth in Germany and by the end of the first lap led by nine seconds. Having won his third drivers' title in 1973 he was preparing to retire after the final race, the

TOP RIGHT: The wide Nürburgring track allowed cars to start four abreast in the 1960s.
RIGHT: Jackie Stewart's Tyrrell en route to victory at Montjuïc Park, Barcelona, in 1971.

Reifen
Continental Reifen
Continental
McLAREN
CLARK
17/115

TOP: Bruce McLaren takes the Monaco Station hairpin in 1969 practice.
ABOVE: The slick-shod Ferrari of Jacky Ickx on the grid at Montjuïc Park in 1971.

USGP at Watkins Glen. When charismatic team-mate François Cevert was killed in practice, the victim of a poorly fitted Armco barrier, he retired on the spot.

In the past, grid spacings had been arranged according to the width of the circuit. In 1950, at Silverstone, cars lined up side by side, 4-3-4, for the opening race. At the next race, Monaco, it was 3-2-3. For the finale at Monza they lined up 4-4-4. It was hardly a great reward for claiming pole to have three cars alongside. From the end of 1973 grids would be 2-2-2, a measure introduced more as a safety precaution to increase the amount of space between cars during the rush towards turn one. From the 1980 season, grids became staggered and today the offset between P1 and P2 is 8 metres.

A new factor ratcheting up lap times was the introduction of slick tyres. They had been used in drag racing but that only required them to be driven straight and not take corners at speed, which required a much stiffer sidewall. In 1971, Firestone introduced slicks for Mario Andretti's Ferrari and by the French Grand Prix, when Jackie Stewart won using Goodyear slicks, the paddock was convinced of their advantage.

Skyscraper wings arrived in 1968 courtesy of F1 designers copying Jim Hall's ground-breaking Chaparral 2E sportscar. The ungainly inverted aerofoils were mounted on spindly struts, front and back, and were adjustable by the driver. They ruined the aesthetics of the cars.

What's more, the high aero load often caused them to collapse, which they did on both Lotus cars over bumps at the Montjuïc Park track in 1969. After first practice in Monaco they were banned, replaced by far lower, less conspicuous rear wings.

But that was not the end of aero experiments. Lotus chief Colin Chapman invested in research on 'ground effect' cars which had inverted aerofoil sidepods. They mimicked the downforce of skyscraper wings but without the drag penalty. And when the sidepods dragged along the ground, the downforce doubled! Lotus experimented with side skirts to seal the vacuum and nearly won with their Lotus 78 in 1977. A year later they had perfected the seal, with Mario Andretti winning six races to become world champion. So now everyone needed a 'ground effect' car. By 1982 the technology had escalated cornering speed to the point that a sudden loss of downforce in a high-speed corner would lead to a frightening accident. Ground effect was outlawed from 1983.

Meanwhile, Brabham owner Bernie Ecclestone, with an eye to where serious money could be made, had organized the independent teams into a lobbying group, FOCA, and wrenched the TV rights from the sport's governing body. Bernie set about forcing television companies to cover all the races in a season or no deal. Formula 1 was about to become mainstream.

TOP RIGHT: François Cevert was tipped as a future world champion before his fatal crash.
RIGHT: Mario Andretti in his Lotus 78 on the rainy tarmac of Île Notre Dame, Montréal.

elf
CEVERT
Ford

John Player
VALVOLINE
John
Player
Special
OLYMPUS
GOOD YEAR
5

25 GITANES
GITANES

ERNATIONAL
Marlboro

THE RISE OF F1 TECHNOLOGY

1982-1993

Bernie Ecclestone's wrangles with motorsport's governing body culminated in the first Concorde Agreement. Named after the FIA's address in Paris, not the harmony both sides achieved, it set out the path Formula 1 would take in the 1980s. It is regularly refined and updated, with the ninth version signed in 2025. Over the next decade, privateer teams running single cars would be banned. From now on, teams were limited to two cars, they needed to build their own chassis, and they had to commit to entering every race. The bar to entering F1 was getting higher and higher. With the rise of expensive turbo engines built by major manufacturers, the bar for success became higher still.

In 1977 Renault had experimented with using 1.5-litre V6 turbo engines, which were fast but prone to breaking down. They had poor driveability, experiencing turbo lag. Most of the British teams still ran 3.0-litre, V8 Cosworth engines, but Ferrari followed Renault's lead in 1981 and Brabham obtained BMW turbos in 1982.

TOP LEFT: A Cosworth V8-powered Ligier and a Renault V6-powered Renault in 1979.
LEFT: McLaren's revolutionary, weight-saving carbon fibre tub.

For so long 'ground effect' had kept the normally aspirated cars in contention, but when it was banned at the end of 1982, it became a turbo championship. McLaren bowed to the inevitable and commissioned Porsche to develop a V6, badged as TAG Turbo, and won successive championships in the hands of Niki Lauda and Alain Prost in 1984 and 1985. Williams struck up a deal with Honda and by the mid 1980s, the Canon-sponsored Williams was slugging it out with McLaren.

Employing carbon fibre to construct chassis also enlarged teams' budgets. McLaren's American engineer Steve Nicholls, using experience gained at Hercules Aerospace, guided designer John Barnard through the build of the first super-light, carbon tub. Paddock sceptics thought it would fragment into a thousand pieces in a high-speed crash. Carbon composite chassis proved to be among the greatest safety advances in the sport's history, along with centrally positioned Kevlar/rubber, sealed-bag fuel cells.

More and more technology was being added to the cars. John Barnard invented the paddle-shift gearbox, first used on the Ferrari 640 in 1989. The semi-automatic system eliminated the need for a clutch pedal and gearstick and allowed the driver to keep two hands on the wheel – a real bonus for tracks like Monaco, requiring up to 50 changes per lap.

TOP RIGHT: The amazingly skillful Gilles Villeneuve in the Ferrari 126CK, 1981.
RIGHT: Nigel Mansell at the wheel of John Barnard's groundbreaking Ferrari 640.

Agip
SINT
TANES
MICHELIN
Agip
27
olivetti

Agip
GOODYEAR
27
Marlboro
FIAT
Agip

obil 1
Mobil 1
Mobil 1
Canon
elf
0
2

Canon
HONDA
calma
ICI
Tactel
Mobil
GOODYEAR
6
Canon

SENNA
NACIONAL

Traction control was first used by Ferrari in 1990, in the form of software connected to a wheel speed sensor. Adopted by all in F1, traction control systems either cut the fuel supply, the spark or closed a fly-by-wire throttle. Starts were easier, too. Launch control eliminated wheelspin off the line giving cars the optimum get-away from the grid. Drivers just had to put their foot down. Braking was easier, too, with ABS eliminating one of the key driver skills.

On top of that, computers were hard at work eliminating pitch and yaw from the suspension of a car. Lotus had pioneered work on 'active ride' in the mid 1980s, with a system that maintained ride height using hydraulic rams with computer-actuated control valves. Williams followed suit, hoping to get maximum aero efficiency from the device. By 1993 Williams engineer Paddy Lowe had vastly improved the technology so that instead of a constant ride height, the car would adjust height to suit the exact corner it was taking. The Williams FW15C which Alain Prost drove to his fourth drivers' title that year remains the most sophisticated F1 car ever produced.

In May 1993, Ayrton Senna, the stand-out driver of his generation, wrote to FIA boss Max Mosley telling him that technology was ruining F1 and eliminating driver skill. Mosley acted. From 1994 the driver aids were taken off the cars.

TOP LEFT: Damon Hill (0) and Alain Prost (2) in F1's most technologically advanced car.
FAR LEFT: Nelson Piquet took victories for the Williams active ride car in 1987.
LEFT: Ayrton Senna, in his final season at McLaren, 1993, was determined F1 should change.

PIRELLI
IBM
WHOOP
GENESYS
UniCredit
hp
hp
Ray-Ban
Ray-Ban
RICHARD MILLE
V-Power

A NEW ERA

QATAR

QUALIFYING

One of the most tinkered-with elements of grand prix racing, qualifying has evolved to its most spectator-friendly form. In the past, qualifying times were recorded on both Friday and Saturday, and if rain arrived on Saturday, no-one went out to risk an accident for zero gain. This was not acceptable in the new, televised era of F1. Also, it was impossible when stretched out over an hour-long session, for TV producers to know when a driver was going to attempt a hot lap.

Various formats were tried. They included 'single lap qualifying' where drivers had one lap, alone on the track, to set their time. From 2006, F1 adopted a three-part knockout system familiar to fans with the ten fastest cars in a Q3 shoot-out. Today, drivers qualify with the bare minimum of fuel, but until the end of 2009 the top ten drivers would qualify with their first stint of fuel on board, so it was tempting to run light and gain a better grid position. That all ended with the 2010 ban on refuelling.

In 2016, the rules were tweaked and drivers were given a five-minute window to set a time, after which the slowest car would drop out (as in velodrome cycling's Elimination Race). It proved to be vastly confusing and lasted two GPs before it, also, was eliminated.

PREVIOUS PAGE: Charles Leclerc leads at the start of the 2026 Australian Grand Prix.
LEFT: Cars line up in the pitlane ahead of Qualifying at Interlagos.

Liberty Media's takeover of the sport's commercial rights in January 2017, brought a new demographic to F1, mostly thanks to the Netflix series *Drive to Survive*. With vast experience of television and new media they wanted to inject different elements into grand prix weekends, something many of the purists and teams had resisted. Covid-19 delayed the plans, but for the 2021 season there would be three Sprint weekends. Instead of three practice sessions on Friday and Saturday there would be one practice on Friday and then qualifying for a sprint race. On Saturday morning there would be the final practice session, followed by the Sprint Qualifying race, which would set the order for the grid on Sunday.

Max Verstappen won the first Sprint Qualifying pole at Silverstone in 2021 (plus the three points on offer), a historic moment that was overshadowed by his clash with Lewis Hamilton at Copse corner in the race the following day. Since then the format has been extended to six events over a season and they are now stand-alone 100 km races with points awarded down to eighth place. They no longer set the grid for Sunday. This means that Sprint weekends now have only one free practice session, two qualifying sessions, a sprint race and a full 305 km grand prix.

TOP RIGHT: One of Max Verstappen's many records – the very first Sprint pole.
RIGHT: Lando Norris scored seven poles in his title-winning year, 2025.
FAR RIGHT: Mercedes driver Kimi Antonelli became the youngest polesitter, at age 19 years and six months, when he claimed P1 for the 2026 Chinese GP.

Red Bull
RACING
33
TAG HEUER
Mobil 1
ORACLE
HONDA
Tezos
1st
Red Bull

allwyn
Android
CISCO
allwyn

TeamViewer
sky sport

TYRE CHOICE

One of the biggest performance differentiators in F1 has been tyres. From 1950 to the end of 2006 there was competition between the likes of Firestone, Goodyear, Bridgestone, Michelin and Pirelli. In the 80s, 90s and early 2000s it seemed like an excuse for F1 to run test teams and burn through money. Shadow squads would pound around European circuits trying to assess the best compound for the races ahead. The Bridgestone vs Michelin battle of 2005 even resulted in a farcical United States GP at Indianapolis, when Bridgestone had advance knowledge of the sidewall stresses endured by the race tyre, while Michelin did not.

In a bid to save money the FIA selected a single tyre supplier in 2007 – Bridgestone until 2011, when Pirelli took over. Their brief is to supply a range of five compounds for slick running and two for wet weather. They range from the hardest, C1, designed for abrasive surfaces such as Bahrain or Silverstone with its high lateral forces, to the softest, C5, used where there is low degradation, often street circuits such as Monaco. Pirelli's task is to create a significant performance gap between each tyre compound (teams are compelled to run two in a dry GP) to make race strategy unpredictable, ideally two-stop races. A Pirelli nightmare is everyone choosing the same tyre strategy for a one-stop race.

TOP: Before 2007, Japanese company Bridgestone produced tyres to suit their leading team.
ABOVE: Pirelli technicians at work on McLaren yellow-walled Medium tyres after practice.

INEOS

VEGAS
LAS
aramco
INEOS
PETRONAS

F1 NIGHT RACES

Singapore's first night race in 2008 heralded a new opportunity for F1. For many years the grands prix in East Asia had fallen outside the time window for core European TV viewing, but the race at Marina Bay proved that scheduling was no longer a problem. It also opened the door for races in ferociously hot climates which could be run in the cool of the evening. The titanium skid plates of the cars sparking on the bumps of the Singapore streets added to the spectacle, even if the first race did finish under the cloud of potential manipulation.

The following season, F1 added its first twilight grand prix in Abu Dhabi, starting at 5pm local time and ending in darkness, with cars threading their way under the ever-changing colours of the Yas Island hotel. Bahrain, the oldest Middle-Eastern GP has switched to a night race (eliminating the rocky outcrop background), alongside Saudi Arabia and Qatar. The most spectacular of all is the Las Vegas Grand Prix, run along the famous Strip with drivers struggling for grip on the cold Nevada tarmac – a wholly different challenge to Singapore where high humidity drains the drivers of energy after two hours in the cockpit.

TOP LEFT: Sparks fly off the Mercedes' titanium skidplate in Singapore.
LEFT: Cars weave past the Sphere on the slippery streets of downtown Las Vegas.

TEAM RADIO

Team Radio was first broadcast in the late 1990s as part of Bernie Ecclestone's pioneering digital pay-per-view TV service. That business folded, but the broadcast of pits-to-driver messages proved popular and became part of the 'live stream' along with suitable delays for editing and bleeping. Rival teams listen just as closely as viewers.

Up until the mid-1980s, communication with the driver was via pitboards giving the barest of details: gaps to cars and lap times. Driver radios started off as one-way, then two-way encrypted and today digital with a stream of information – sometimes unwelcome – passed over.

Following the team orders ban from 2002 to 2010, race control listened closely to team messages that might be construed as a race-changing instruction, most famously in 2010 when Ferrari engineer Rob Smedley informed his driver Felipe Massa that: 'Fernando is faster than you...sorry.' In other words, 'move over'.

There was also an F1 directive aimed at limiting driver coaching, with teams reprimanded for telling drivers where they could improve on a lap mid race. The latest rule changes from 2026 demand a high degree of energy manipulation around a lap and have made the drivers' jobs more complex than ever, and so team radio has never been more important.

ABOVE: Engineer Rob Smedley with Ferrari driver Felipe Massa.

ABOVE: The halo viewed from above on the 2018 Haas.

THE HALO

Formula 1 had long been aware of the dangers posed by errant wheels cast loose in accidents on track, either hitting spectators or other cars. The wheel tethers introduced in 1998 to keep them attached could still be severed in massive accidents. The dangers were put into sharp focus in 2009, when Henry Surtees, son of former world champion John Surtees, was killed at Brands Hatch in an F2 race by a wheel bouncing high and crashing straight back down onto his cockpit. In addition, through the history of F1, drivers had suffered horrific injuries from cars penetrating poorly secured Armco barriers, including François Cevert, the team-mate Jackie Stewart tipped to be a future world champion, after a gruesome accident at Watkins Glen.

Caught in the spotlight of Jules Bianchi's avoidable accident at Suzuka in 2014, when his Marussia hit a recovery vehicle, the sport's governing body, the FIA, set about finding a safety solution. Together with Mercedes they developed a titanium bar attached to the car in three places known as the 'halo'. Drivers hated it. Lewis Hamilton described it as 'the worst-looking mod in F1 history', although he was persuaded by an FIA presentation that revealed a 17 per cent increased chance of accident survival.

There was opposition on multiple grounds: it restricted visibility, made it more difficult to extract drivers in an accident, looked unsightly, even made the cars look 'too safe'. Max Verstappen believed it made F1 cars 'safer than riding a bicycle in a city.' Haas driver Romain Grosjean hated it. Nevertheless it was introduced in 2018 and immediately proved to be a valuable safety addition, especially in the 2018 Belgian Grand Prix where Nico Hülkenberg locked his brakes into the first turn, rear-ended Fernando Alonso's McLaren, launching it over Charles Leclerc's Sauber. Teams liked it because it introduced more 'high visibility' space to sell advertising.

The halo saved Lewis Hamilton from a career-ending injury at Monza in 2021 when Max Verstappen made a clumsy lunge into the first chicane and ended with his wheel compressing Lewis's helmet, protected by the aptly-named halo. And few can forget the dramatic scenes at Bahrain in 2020, when Romain Grosjean's Haas speared through the barrier and left the driver struggling to get out of his car and the engulfing flames for 28 seconds. Without the halo, he would have already been dead.

TOP RIGHT: Max Verstappen's rear wheel impacts Hamilton's helmet at Monza in 2021.
RIGHT: The burning remnants of Romain Grosjean's Haas at the Bahrain GP.

HONDA
E:TECHNOLOGY
CROWDSTRIKE
AMG

VGW
PLAY
38
aws
Palantir
PIRELLI
CELSIUS
Santander
V-Power

SIMULATORS

Where once there was an F1 test team, now there is a Driver-in-the-Loop simulation team with dedicated simulator drivers. They are far more than a handy tool to allow new drivers to learn a track. Huge investments have been made to correlate the simulator and the real car, so that 'the sim' handles exactly like the race car on the track.

The ease at which teenage rookies can now step into a car was demonstrated by F2 runner Ollie Bearman's debut at the 2024 Saudi Arabian Grand Prix, when he was a last-minute replacement for Ferrari's Carlos Sainz at the tricky Jeddah Corniche circuit. He finished seventh on debut.

Cockpits are identical to the real car and tracks are modelled in minute detail, factoring in kerbs, bumps and surface type. In the week, the Sim will run new development parts to see if they add speed or downforce to the car. On grand prix weekends, data is transmitted back to the team base, and set-up changes run on the simulator to see if they can improve the pace in between practice sessions. One of Adrian Newey's key requirements when he joined Aston Martin from Red Bull was that they improve the Driver-in-the-Loop simulator, such is the vital part they play in setting up the car.

LEFT: Ollie Bearman is wheeled into position on the Saudi Arabian grid in 2024. The Ferrari reserve driver made an impressive debut thanks to his time in 'the Sim'.

2026 TECH RULES

The changes to the technical regulations at the beginning of the 2026 season were widely regarded as the biggest in history, with new aero, engines, fuel and tyres. McLaren team principal Andrea Stella described them as 'unprecedented'. With no carry-over from the 2025 cars, everyone was starting from scratch.

Cars were smaller (10cm narrower and 20cm shorter), lighter (30kg), and more environmentally friendly (fully sustainable fuels). The DRS, the precious aid to overtaking had gone, replaced with 'overtake' buttons to attack and 'boost' buttons to defend. Now with a 50/50 split in energy from combustion and electrical energy, it was going to be battery management that helped drivers find a way past the car in front. Drivers would need to start thinking like Formula E competitors.

With a potential loss of overall power, the FIA didn't want an unenviable comparison with F2 speeds and so the design shackles were taken off movable aerodynamics, while the Venturi floors of 2022-2025 were also ditched. The engines remained 1.6-litre V6 turbo hybrids, but now with only MGU-K energy, and engine braking used for 'super clipping' to harvest more precious electrical energy. It was a brave new world of road-relevant tech that would have obvious winners and losers.

ABOVE: Two 'renders' released by the FIA to show the 2026 design parameters.

TOP: George Russell's complex Mercedes steering wheel in 2026.
ABOVE In 2026, wing lights reveal a driver's energy harvesting through the lap.

ENERGY DEPLOYMENT

The 2026 season marked a radical departure in energy deployment with a 50/50 split between electrical power and the internal combustion engine (ICE). Max Verstappen called it 'Formula E on steroids' describing the new formula in caustic terms as one of careful battery management as opposed to flat-out racing. It demanded a completely new style of driving. Before, drivers had to manage their tyres and their fuel load. Now they would have to work out the most efficient places to press the boost and harvest buttons.

On some of the longest straights, especially Las Vegas and Baku, there was a real danger of running out of energy, given the harvesting limits. New start procedures were also needed to allow drivers to 'spool up' their turbos – with ten seconds needed for those at the back of the grid to ramp up to full power.

After three races, the heavily criticized rules were amended to increase the amount of energy harvesting during a lap to increase electrical power. Then, in May, it was announced that fuel flow on the ICE would be increased for 2027, making it closer to a 60/40 split and boost speeds.

LVMH
Paramount+
LANDMAN
NEW SEASON
HONDA
Red Bull
ORACLE
PETRONAS
TeamViewer
aramco
cognizant
14
18
KICK
BWT
HUGO
Red Bull
Cash App
VISA
30

TEAMS

PREVIOUS PAGE: The cars in Parc Fermé after Abu Dhabi qualifying 2025.
ABOVE: Gilles Villeneuve (27) alongside Dider Pironi in the Imola pit lane, 1981.

FERRARI

Though names like Alfa Romeo, Mercedes and Lotus come and go in Formula 1, Ferrari have always been there. They may have missed the first race – and odd races when Enzo Ferrari deemed it too expensive to travel – but they are the oldest F1 team by over a decade.

Having started in motorsport running Alfa Romeos, from 1950 the 'Scuderia' were an F1 constructor and competitor, winning drivers' titles with Alberto Ascari in 1952 and 1953, and then Juan Manuel Fangio in 1956. Fangio left after one season of feeling under-appreciated, a response that would be shared by Niki Lauda in 1977. There were further titles for Mike Hawthorn in 1958 and Phil Hill in 1961, with the beautiful Ferrari 156 'sharknose' finally proving that the Italian team could build rear-engined cars.

The 1960s and early 1970s were dominated by the English 'garagistes' with their Cosworth V8 engines, until Ferrari hired the aristocratic Luca Cordero di Montezemolo as team manager. He brought in Niki Lauda, who took the Mauro Forghieri-designed Ferrari 312T to world championships in 1975 and 1977, only falling short in 1976 in the downpour of Mount Fuji.

Ferrari managed a further drivers' title with Jody Scheckter in 1979 and constructors' titles in 1982 and 1983, despite the tragic loss of Gilles Villeneuve and a career-ending injury to Didier Pironi in 1982. Otherwise the 80s and 90s were a barren spell – neither Alain Prost or Nigel Mansell could win a championship and the team were so short of ideas they hired former-McLaren designer John Barnard, who insisted he work from Guildford.

Montezemolo had long since left the company, but his return in the 1990s sparked the Ferrari renaissance. He hired the first non-Italian team boss, Jean Todt, along with technical director Ross Brawn, chief designer Rory Byrne and, most important of all, Michael Schumacher. With a huge budget and a test track, Fiorano, on their doorstep they re-wrote the Ferrari record book, winning six constructors' and five drivers' titles between 1999 and 2004.

Todt's insistence on team orders, despite Schumacher dominance, had a negative impact on the sport, and team orders were banned after a farcical Austrian Grand Prix of 2002. Fernando Alonso and Renault finally put a stop to Michael's winning ways – and though new driver Kimi Räikkönen gained a last-race title in 2007, Felipe Massa lost out on the last lap in 2008 – a fate repeated by Fernando Alonso in 2010 and 2012.

The arrival of the hybrid era in 2014 has seen them trail Mercedes-engined cars and even with the stellar talents of Lewis Hamilton and Charles Leclerc behind the wheel, the political machinations of Italy's heavily scrutinized team have held them back.

TOP: Michael Schumacher takes the Swimming Pool chicane at Monaco in 2003.
ABOVE: Lewis Hamilton in 2026's Ferrari SF-26.

TOP: In 1988 Ayrton Senna was leading the Monaco GP by 50 seconds when he crashed out.
ABOVE: Kimi Räikkönen leads team-mate Juan Pablo Montoya in 2005.

McLAREN

The inspirational driver-engineer Bruce McLaren formed his eponymous team in 1963 to go racing through the winter months in his native New Zealand. He had been driving in F1 for the Cooper team since 1959 but finally stepped into one of his own cars at the 1966 Monaco Grand Prix. His first GP win came at Spa in 1968, although the greater part of the team's early success was in the Can-Am sportscar series in North America. It was testing one of these cars at Goodwood in 1970 that the 'safest' of drivers lost his life, when a piece of bodywork broke loose, sending the car out of control.

Team manager Teddy Mayer took over the reins. Under his stewardship Yardley became the team's first title sponsor in 1972, followed by Marlboro in 1974, the year that Emerson Fittipaldi clinched his second drivers' title and McLaren's first constructors' trophy.

The Marlboro sponsorship lasted 23 years, from 1974 to 1996 and the iconic red and white livery became associated with McLaren, especially in the dominant Prost/Senna era of the 1980s. Prior to that James Hunt had won a memorable championship for McLaren in 1976, but his 1977 win at Mount Fuji was the last for some time. Ron Dennis took control of the struggling team for the 1981 season by merging it with his Project

Four Racing organization, transforming McLaren into a technologically advanced hotbed for designers Steve Nicholls, Gordon Murray, Neil Oatley and John Barnard.

The 1980s and early 1990s brought unprecedented success with uneasy team-mates Senna and Prost pushing each other – occasionally off the track. Honda had provided the engine powering their success, but when they quit the sport in the midst of the Japanese asset bubble crisis, the team were left floundering. It was only the arrival of Mercedes engines and designer Adrian Newey that brought them more titles for Mika Häkkinen in 1998 and 1999.

Losing out to Ferrari during Schumacher's reign there, McLaren had a resurgence with Lewis Hamilton almost clinching a title in his debut season of 2007, finally bringing it home in 2008. With Mercedes entering the sport themselves in 2010, Ron Dennis took the view that he was never going to win titles with a customer engine and set about acquiring a Honda return. The engine was a disaster, Fernando Alonso called it a 'GP2 engine' and Dennis was forced out of the company he had done so much to build.

Incoming boss Zak Brown, for a long time McLaren's sponsorship fixer, renewed the Mercedes deal and finally returned them to winning ways with a constructors' title in 2024 (the first since 1998) and both titles in a nailbiting 2025 finale.

TOP: In 2007 Lewis Hamilton almost became a rookie world champion.
ABOVE: World champion Lando Norris in the McLaren MCL40.

ABOVE: In 1993 the incredibly sophisticated Williams FW15C took Alain Prost to his fourth and final drivers' title.

WILLIAMS

Frank Williams was a regular face in the paddock through the early 1970s, running privateers on a shoestring, including the late Piers Courage. It was his partnership with engineer Patrick Head to form Williams Grand Prix Engineering that reversed his fortunes. The team's breakthrough came in 1979 with the 'ground effect' Williams FW07, which in the hands of rugged Australian driver Alan Jones won four of the last six grands prix of 1979. Momentum carried through to 1980 with five wins and the drivers' title. His team-mate, the enigmatic Carlos Reutemann, had the chance to win again in 1981 but lost out to Nelson Piquet in the final race at Caesars Palace, Las Vegas. Ironically it was Williams' Keke Rosberg who won the following year in that same dusty car park, having amassed just one win and 44 points in the season. It should have been Ferrari's Didier Pironi but the Frenchman had broken both legs in a practice accident at Hockenheim.

In 1984 the team received Honda engines, which proved to be the class of the field. However drivers Nigel Mansell and new team-mate Nelson Piquet didn't get on. Either of them could have won the 1986 drivers' title but with Mansell leading the final race in Adelaide, a spectacular blow-out on the Brabham straight handed the trophy to Alain Prost.

Piquet won the following year, taking his Honda engine supply to Lotus. The team also had to adapt to Frank Williams' disability in 1986 after a road car accident left him wheelchair bound.

It was not until the team took on Renault V10 engines and designer Adrian Newey that their fortunes reversed. Newey's Leyton House cars had punched well above their weight, and the combination of his design talent, the Renault engine and advanced electronics created some of the most sophisticated F1 machinery. Mansell won in 1992, Prost in 1993, Senna (who offered his services free) or Hill should have won for Williams in 1994, but the Imola tragedy and Schumacher gamesmanship intervened. Hill bounced back to claim the 1996 drivers' title, followed by Jacques Villeneuve in 1997.

But 1997 was the year when the succession of constructors' titles came to an abrupt end. The early 2000s saw a brief resurgence with BMW engines – Juan Pablo Montoya and Ralf Schumacher delivered race wins, but when BMW left the sport in 2005 it was back to square one. From then on it was a gradual slipping to the back of the grid, punctuated by odd moments of success, especially when Mercedes hybrid engines were the thing to have. Frank passed control of the team to his daughter Claire Williams, who supervised the takeover by Dorilton Capital in 2020. Incoming team principal James Vowles is looking to reverse the many years of under-investment and return the team to the top step of the podium.

TOP: Carlos Reutemann narrowly failed to win the 1981 championship in the FW07C.
ABOVE: Carlos Sainz in the Williams FW48 in 2026.

TOP: The all-conquering Mercedes W05 from 2014.
ABOVE: Kimi Antonelli at the wheel of the 2026 Mercedes-AMG W17.

MERCEDES

A Mercedes team has enjoyed two dominant periods in Formula 1. Led by the formidable Alfred Neubauer in the mid 1950s it was regularly scoring grand prix 1-2s with Juan-Manuel Fangio and Stirling Moss. But after the Mercedes sportscar of Pierre Levegh crashed at Le Mans in 1955, killing 82 people, they withdrew from the sport.

Mercedes had bought a stake in British-based engine company Ilmor in the 1990s, gradually increasing its ownership to form Mercedes-Ilmor in 2002, eventually becoming the wholly owned Mercedes AMG High Performance Powertrains. Having powered McLaren to world championship trophies – and both titles for Brawn in 2009 – they acquired Ross Brawn's squad and hired Michael Schumacher to finish his career as he'd started – in a Mercedes race car.

The early years with Nico Rosberg were less than stellar, but the hiring of Lewis Hamilton in 2013 was a portent of results to come. The introduction of hybrid engines in 2014 made them the most dominant F1 team yet, winning both titles from 2014 to 2020. A failed concept for the new rules shift saw their success drop away from 2022 along with increasing friction between team boss Toto Wolff and Red Bull rival Christian Horner.

RED BULL

Long-time F1 sponsor, Red Bull founder Dietrich Mateschitz took the leap and bought his own team in 2005. He picked up the failing Jaguar F1 team and installed Christian Horner as team boss on a recommendation from fellow Austrian Dr Helmut Marko. The team's aim was to put the 'fun' back into F1, but Horner set about hiring 'the most competitive man' that McLaren boss Ron Dennis had ever met – Adrian Newey.

Newey struggled with the old Jaguar mindset at first, but by 2009 had produced a championship-winning car ... except Brawn had stolen a march on the teams that year with their double diffuser. By the time Red Bull added one to the RB5 it was too late. The RB6 was the first of four title-winning cars for Sebastian Vettel from 2010 to 2013.

The hybrid engine Renault had built for 2014 was severely underpowered compared to its rivals, with the despairing Horner opting for Honda engines from 2019. The rules re-set in 2022 gave an advantage to the one man with experience of Venturi floors – Newey – and with the generational talent of Max Verstappen behind the wheel they re-wrote the grand prix record books in 2022 and 2023. However Mateschitz's death in 2022 created a power struggle within the team which led to the exit of Newey, Horner and Helmut Marko, to make way for Laurent Mekies – an engineer refocusing the team in the new hybrid era.

TOP: Max Verstappen at the wheel of the record-breaking Red Bull-Honda RB19 in 2023.
ABOVE: The 2026 Red Bull-Ford ditched the matt blue finish of previous years.

ABOVE: The wide airbox of the VCARB03 is a striking feature of the 2026 car.

RACING BULLS

Red Bull's junior team, RB, started life as Minardi in 1985, in Faenza, Italy. Giancarlo Minardi's back-of-the-grid strugglers won admiration for their persistence rather than their (complete lack of) results. Often the first step into F1 for top drivers, Fernando Alonso and Mark Webber drove for the team before stepping into faster machinery. When Dietrich Mateschitz bought the team in 2005 that is exactly what he had planned for the reborn 'Scuderia Toro Rosso'. The Faenza team would take young drivers from Helmut Marko's Red Bull young driver programme to give them experience before the step up to the senior team, Red Bull Racing.

Sebastian Vettel, Carlos Sainz and Daniel Ricciardo all came through the programme, Vettel even managing to embarrass the senior squad by winning for Toro Rosso at Monza, before Red Bull had scored a victory. It was the offer of a Toro Rosso drive that clinched Max Verstappen's signature when Mercedes were poised to sign him in 2014.

The team was rebranded in 2020 to promote Red Bull's fashion brand Alpha Tauri, then four years later took the money and rebranded as Visa Cash App RB, a surefire way to crush fan engagememt. Long-standing Austrian team boss Franz Tost retired, handing over the reins to Laurent Mekies in 2023 before his promotion to the senior team.

cognizant
aramco
cognizant
14
aramco
aramco
cognizant

aramco
18
BOSS
Xerox
NetApp
aramco
aramco

ASTON MARTIN

Aston Martin is the latest incarnation of what was the Jordan team. Charismatic Irishman and full-time member of F1's 'Piranha Club' Eddie Jordan converted his F3000 team to F1 in 1991. He kept the team afloat by a succession of wily deals, often helped with finances by F1 supremo Bernie Ecclestone. He sold out in 2005 to Midland (for one season) becoming Spyker (for one season), before Indian entrepreneur Vijay Mallya took over and the team became Force India from 2008 to 2018.

Though Jordan had won races with Damon Hill and Giancarlo Fisichella, Force India were solidly 'mid grid'. Canadian businessman Laurence Stroll, who had long financed his son Lance's driving career, bought the team, which ran as Racing Point at first. Stroll Senior added the carmaker to his portfolio and rebranded the F1 team as Aston Martin in 2021. He then set about an enormous investment programme at Jordan's old Silverstone factory, hiring and firing some of the best names in the sport – drafting in Sebastian Vettel and Fernando Alonso to partner his son. The highest profile signing was F1's most successful designer of all time, Adrian Newey – and it was quite fitting that Eddie Jordan negotiated the deal.

TOP LEFT: Fernando Alonso's first season at Aston Martin yielded eight podiums.
LEFT: Lance Stroll locks up in Bahrain 2026, during testing.

ALPINE

The Alpine F1 Team has motorsport roots stretching back to 1981 and the Toleman team. Benetton bought the squad in 1986 and moved their base to Enstone in the Cotswolds. Under the guidance of commercial director Flavio Briatore, and technical director Ross Brawn, Michael Schumacher won back-to-back championships in 1994 and 1995. Fernando Alonso repeated the feat in 2005 and 2006 by which time the team had been bought by Renault.

A lack of results in 2008 caused the notorious 'Crashgate' scandal when Nelson Piquet Jr crashed deliberately to hand team-mate Fernando Alonso a strategic advantage and victory. Briatore was subsequently banned from the sport.

When Genii Capital became a major shareholder in 2012 they rebranded the team as Lotus F1 Team, before Renault re-entered the fray for 2016. By this time, the paddock had taken to calling it 'Team Enstone' to avoid confusion.

From 2021 Renault decided to promote its sports brand Alpine by attaching the name to Team Enstone. After waves of senior staff changes were instigated by the French company, Flavio Briatore returned as an 'advisor' and took the unprecedented step of ditching Renault engines, securing a Mercedes power unit for 2026.

TOP: Fernando Alonso won his two world titles for Renault in 2005 and 2006.
ABOVE: For 2026 Alpine took the radical step of ditching Renault engines.

AUDI

For many years there was talk of the Volkswagen-Audi Group entering F1 and they finally took the plunge by buying Swiss motorsport grandee Peter Sauber's team. Sauber had enjoyed partnerships with Mercedes, BMW and Ferrari during a storied F1 career that began in 1993 with Karl Wendlinger and JJ Lehto behind the wheel.

Approaching retirement he sold the team, based in Hinwill, Switzerland, to the Audi brand of VAG. They had finally been lured into the sport by the prospect of building their own hybrid engine with a large emphasis on energy recovery – knowledge that would be road car relevant. They also had the heritage of the iconic pre-war Auto-Unions of Bernd Rosemeyer and Tazio Nuvolari.

Audi employed ex-Ferrari team principal Mattia Binotto, an engine specialist, to guide what was already an experienced F1 team. The driver line-up for the debut 2026 season of Audi Revolut featured a blend of experience, Nico Hülkenberg, with rising Brazilian star Gabriel Bortoleto in his second year on the grid. Their ambitious goal of targeting a world championship by 2030 may prove hard to achieve, not least because Switzerland is an expensive place to run an F1 team from in the face of a restrictive budget cap.

RIGHT (BOTH): Audi's first F1 car, the R26, in the hands of Nico Hülkenberg.

bp
Castrol
Revolut
NEXO
ninjaOne
visit
QATAR

TOP: Romain Grosjean in Haas's strong debut season, 2016.
ABOVE: Ferrari academy graduate Ollie Berman in the 2026 Haas.

HAAS

American-led teams had struggled in F1 prior to Gene Haas's arrival on the grid in 2016. The pragmatic NASCAR owner took the wise option of buying as much of his car as regulations allowed – the engine and gearbox from Ferrari and the chassis design and manufacturing by single-seater experts Dallara. In charge he put plain-speaking boss Guenther Steiner, a veteran of the Jaguar and Red Bull teams, who hired experienced drivers Kevin Magnussen and Romain Grosjean.

By 2018 they had risen to an incredible 5th, beating long-established teams McLaren, Williams and Sauber. It became a popular team thanks to the Netflix series *Drive to Survive*, which was initially shunned by the top teams and so concentrated on the under-pressure Steiner and his awkward post-race phone calls to Gene Haas.

After five seasons together the Magnussen/Grosjean partnership was dissolved in 2021 in favour of income from rookie pay-drivers Mick Schumacher and Nikita Mazepin, who proceeded to hit each other on track and cause expensive accident damage. The following season they rehired Kevin Magnussen. There was much disappointment from Netflix when Haas did not renew Steiner's contract in 2024 and his more carefully spoken engineer Ayao Komatsu took charge.

ABOVE: Employing experienced drivers such as Sergio Perez (pictured) and Valtteri Bottas has given Cadillac a reliable base line to develop from.

CADILLAC

For many years FIA boss Max Mosley was wary of having large manufacturer teams in F1 – Toyota, Honda, BMW had all quit the sport when the world financial markets collapsed. But such is the global impetus of F1 in the 2020s that only the largest of corporations can fund an entirely new team.

Michael Andretti, son of world champion Mario, put together a bid that convinced the sport's governing body that an 11th team was viable, but the commercial rights holder, Formula One Management, thought otherwise. The existing teams saw a dilution of the prize money and the likelihood they would lose all-American sponsors. But when General Motors put their financial muscle and the Cadillac brand behind the team (along with the sidelining of Andretti) the bid was accepted.

Based at Silverstone, former Marussia boss Graeme Lowdon was able to assemble an experienced team of engineers. Cadillac followed the Haas route and opted for Ferrari power units while it focuses on building its own engine, potentially for 2029. For its inaugural season, the team chose experienced drivers Sergio Perez and Valtteri Bottas, with former Alfa Romeo driver Zhou Guanyu as reserve. The team hope to bring in American driver Colton Herta once he earns enough superlicence points by competing in Formula 2.

EXPLORA
JOURNEYS
MONACO

LEGENDARY CIRCUITS

SILVERSTONE

Formula 1 started here – but not with the British Grand Prix. The debut race for motor sport's top series was officially the Royal Automobile Club's Grand Prix d'Europe, a nod to the fact that Britain had been late to the party compared to Italy, Germany and France, countries that had dominated pre-war road racing. Silverstone was largely formed of the perimeter roads of RAF Silverstone, a wartime training base for Wellington bombers. Famous corners, such as Woodcote, Copse, Becketts and Stowe were part of the original layout and what is now the Wellington Straight was once a runway for Vickers' finest aircraft.

Unlike contemporaries Monza, Spa and Monaco, which all hosted races in 1950, Silverstone has constantly updated its circuit, most notably with the challenging, fast sweepers of the Maggots/Becketts complex in 1991, the addition of Vale corner, modification of the Luffield chicane to slow cars through Woodcote (scene of a multiple car pile-up in 1973).

Having been constantly pressured by F1 supremo Bernie Ecclestone and FIA boss Max Mosley to upgrade its facilities – or suffer the loss of the grand prix – owners the British Racing Drivers' Club finally took action.

PREVIOUS PAGE: Monaco's Fairmont hairpin is the tightest corner in F1.

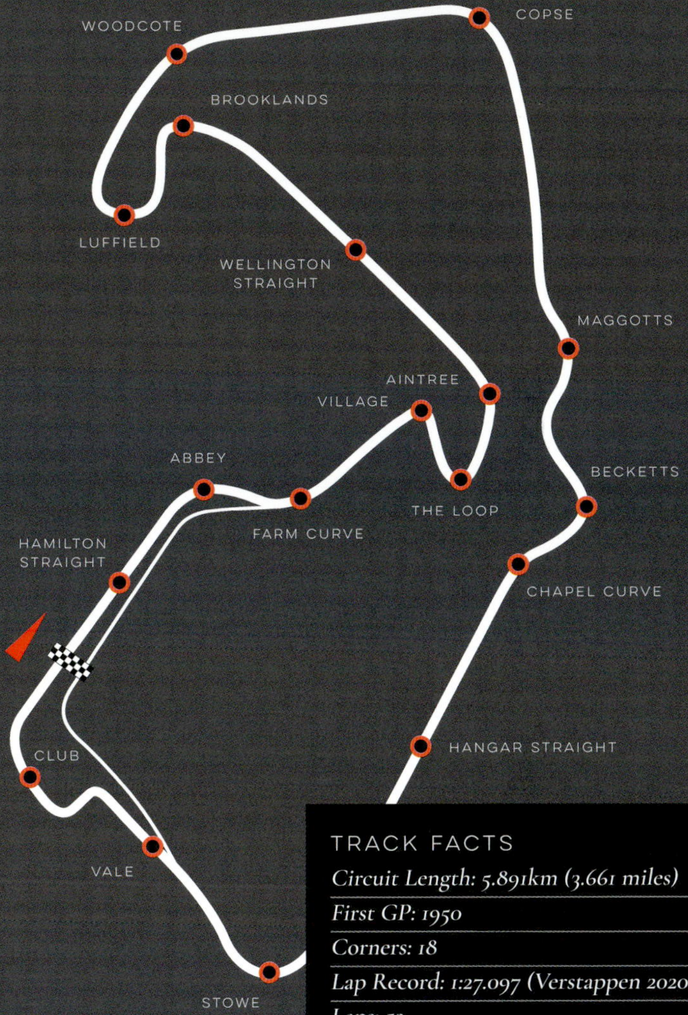

TRACK FACTS

Circuit Length: 5.891km (3.661 miles)

First GP: 1950

Corners: 18

Lap Record: 1:27.097 (Verstappen 2020)

Laps: 52

Direction: Clockwise

The start/finish straight was moved to just after Club corner, and new corners such as Village, The Loop and Aintree were added to lengthen the circuit and add opportunities for wheel-to-wheel racing in the opening third of the lap. The magnificent Wing building now presides over the start line on the Hamilton Straight, the only track element named after a driver.

NOTABLE RACES

1973: Jackie Stewart's Tyrrell skids and disappears into the barley crop with only the airbox visible.

1985: Williams' Keke Rosberg sets the first ever 160mph qualifying lap in a Williams.

1991: Nigel Mansell wins the 1991 GP and gives rival Ayrton Senna a lift back on the side of his car.

1999: Michael Schumacher breaks his leg as his Ferrari's brakes fail before Stowe corner and he runs straight on into the tyre barrier.

2000: Max Mosley schedules the British GP for April and the grass car parks turn to a muddy quagmire.

2021: Max Verstappen collides with Lewis Hamilton at the 160mph Copse corner and spins off.

2022: Zhou Guanyu escapes unharmed after a startline accident hurtles his Sauber upside down along the track.

TOP RIGHT: The Alfa Romeo of Zhou Guanyu about to test the load-bearing capacity of its roll hoop at the start of the 2022 race. It stood up to the crash test.
RIGHT: Lewis Hamilton approaches Club corner in 2025 with the Wing building beyond.

Heineken -0.0-
Heineken -0.0- Heineken -0.0- Heineken -0.0-
QATAR AIRWAYS

CIRCUIT DE MONACO

It is the most famous grand prix in the world, but the unique challenge of Monaco puts overtaking at a premium and ensures that Saturday qualifying is more important than the race on Sunday.

In the 1920s, Monaco resident and head of the Automobile Club, Anthony Noghès, wanted to add a grand prix to the existing Monte Carlo rally, but needed to plot a course through the city (unlike the rally which wound through Southern France). The circuit he devised is essentially still in place. It has gained a tunnel and lost a railway station (next to the slowest corner in F1, the Old Station/Fairmont hairpin) but, most importantly, gained more than straw bales along the harbour front. Over the years, two cars have ended up in the Mediterranean but neither driver was seriously injured.

Reclamation of land from the harbour allowed the incredibly cramped pits to be enlarged in 2003, but not by much, especially when the Cadillac team was squeezed in for 2026. It is still the most glamorous F1 circuit and also the most visceral experience for F1 spectators, sitting just metres away at the breathtakingly fast Swimming Pool complex. Traditionally it was the F1 race where most sponsor business was done, but that mantle may be slipping to Miami.

TRACK FACTS

Circuit Length: 3.337km (2.074 miles)

First GP: 1929 – First F1 GP: 1950

Corners: 19

Lap Record: 1:12.909 (Hamilton 2021)

Laps: 78

Direction: Clockwise

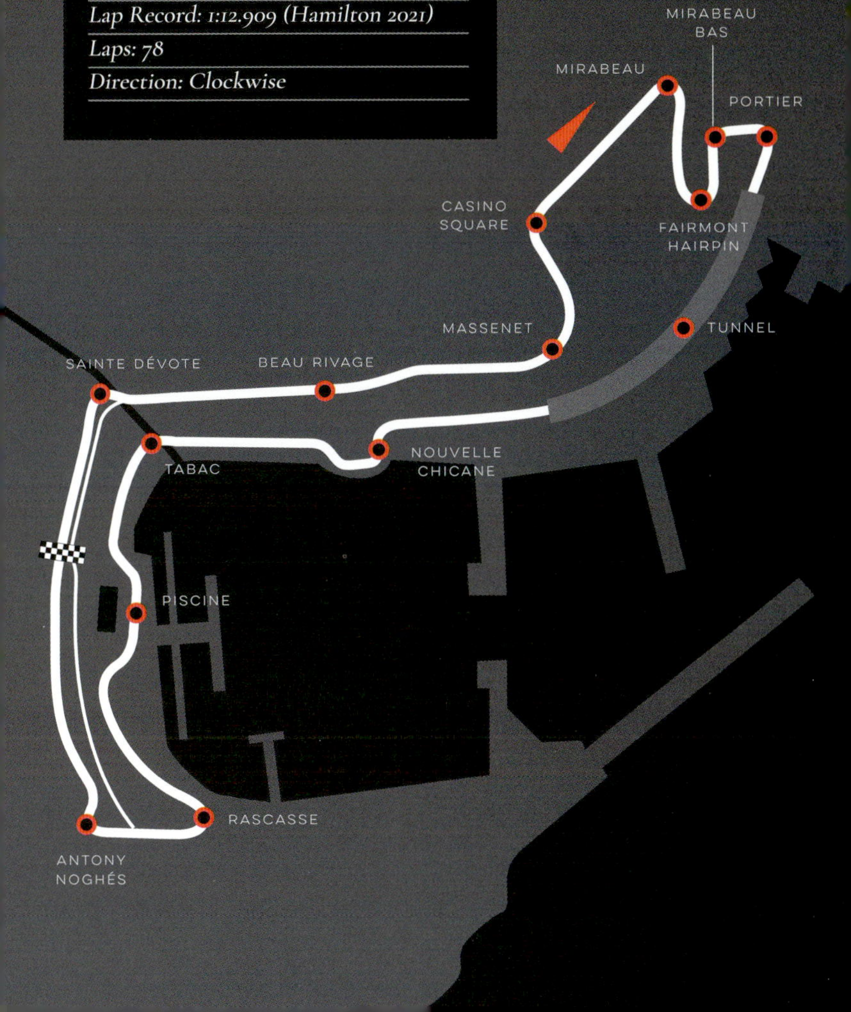

TAG HEUER
TAGHeuer
TAGHeuer

NOTABLE RACES

1933: Monaco becomes the first grand prix to have a grid ordered by practice times.

1967: Lorenzo Bandini perishes after his car catches fire on the exit of the Nouvelle chicane.

1969: The ugly and dangerous 'skyscraper' wings are banned after practice.

1970: Jack Brabham loses the race at the final corner of the final lap when he slides into the Armco, allowing Jochen Rindt to win.

1982: 'The Race Nobody Wanted To Win.' Alain Prost, Didier Pironi, Andrea de Cesaris and Derek Daly all lead in the final few laps, but then crash, run out of fuel, suffer engine problems etc. Ricardo Patrese spins on oil, but manages to bump start his car. He has no idea he has won when he crosses the line.

1984: Ayrton Senna's heroic pursuit of Alain Prost in the wet ends when the race is red-flagged early.

2006: Michael Schumacher 'parks' his Ferrari, spinning at the 40mph Rascasse corner in qualifying to prevent Fernando Alonso from grabbing pole.

2024: Monegasque Charles Leclerc finally wins his home grand prix.

TOP LEFT: Lando Norris locks up his McLaren brakes at Ste. Dévote in the 2025 grand prix.
LEFT: The stretch from Tabac corner through to the Swimming Pool/Piscine is one of the most exhilarating places to watch an F1 car in action.

SPA-FRANCORCHAMPS

Drivers' favourite Spa-Francorchamps was originally 14.98 km in length and run entirely on public roads. Starting at La Source, the circuit headed down over the Eau Rouge river, up the hill past Raidillon and out into the countryside of Malmedy, before taking a turn downhill at great speed through the Masta Kink, turning right at Stavelot, then another long drag down to the finish line between La Source hairpin and Eau Rouge.

Spa already had a reputation for danger, claiming the life of pre-war Mercedes driver Richard Seaman in 1939, but the 1960 Belgian Grand Prix was the blackest day in F1, when two British drivers were killed within fifteen minutes of each other. The rain-sodden 1966 race saw half the field exit on the first lap, including Jackie Stewart and Graham Hill, who spun off at the Masta Kink. Stewart had to be rescued by his fellow drivers, an event that galvanized him into a lifelong safety drive. The race was boycotted by the drivers in 1969.

Spa gave way to the Nivelles circuit and then Zolder before the new Spa emerged in 1979. The greatly shortened track had cut out the fearsome Burnenville

TRACK FACTS

Circuit Length: 7.004km (4.352 miles)

First GP: 1925 – First F1 GP: 1950

Corners: 19

Lap Record: 1:44.701 (Perez 2024)

Laps: 44

Direction: Clockwise

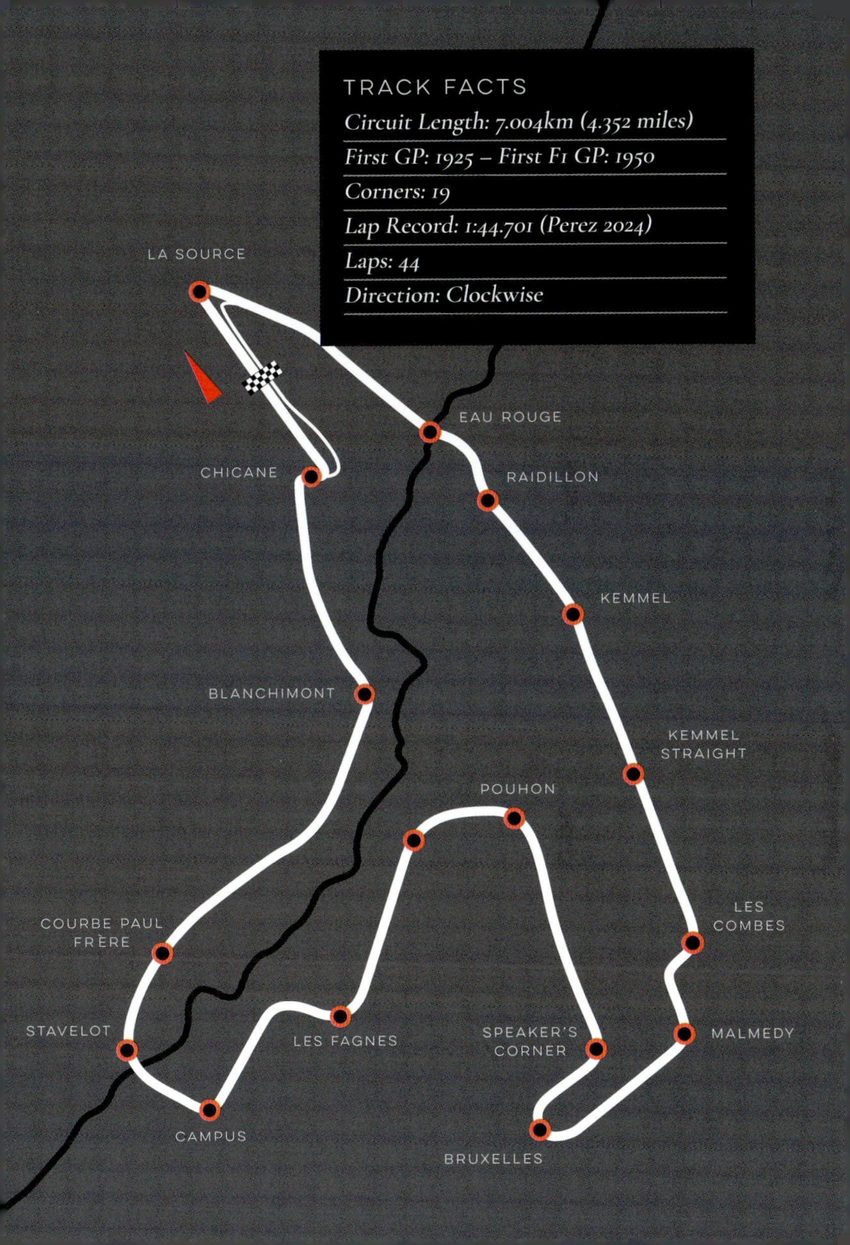

TOP: Cars stream down towards Eau Rouge at the start of the 2025 GP.
ABOVE: Charles Leclerc rounds La Source hairpin, one of the original corners.

and Masta, instead turning right at the top of the hill after Les Combes and flowing downhill through a series of challenging turns, Pouhon and Fagnes, before rejoining the circuit above Blanchimont. F1 made a return in 1983 and there was universal praise for the new layout. It had retained the atmosphere and challenge of the old Spa, yet provided the safety standards demanded of the 1980s. Both Eau Rouge/Raidillon and Blanchimont are two of F1's fastest corners, made easier by the Venturi floors of 2022-25, but trickier now with the 2026 regulations. Spa's on/off relationship with the F1 calendar is more to do with investment from the race organizers than the rain which often arrives on a GP weekend.

NOTABLE RACES

1966: Only seven of the 16 cars make it through to the second lap. All three BRMs have accidents.

1991: Jordan is paid £150,000 by Mercedes to give their protégé Michael Schumacher a one-off race and is then snapped up by Benetton.

1998: Schumacher turns his Ferrari into a three-wheeler and storms down the pit lane to confront the driver he hit, David Coulthard.

2015: Max Verstappen makes an outlandish overtaking move on Felipe Nasr at Blanchimont and wins the FIA's 'Action of the Year' award.

MONZA

Known as the Temple of Speed, the *pista magica* and the Cathedral of Motorsport, Monza's official name, Autodrome Nazionale, was intended as a slight to Rome, but it is apt. The national expectation of Ferrari and its passionate fans, *tifosi*, to do well at Monza comes into sharp focus every year. It was built in Monza's Royal Park in the 1920s, combining a road racing track and a banked concrete oval, emulating Britain's Brooklands (1907).

But the bumpy concrete proved dangerous and a car breaker, killing three drivers on Black Sunday in 1933. The initial four runnings of the F1 Italian Grand Prix took place solely on the road course, but there was an option to run a combined course – one lap of the road course followed by one lap of the oval. This took its final bow for the 1960 and 1961 grands prix, solely because it favoured engine power (Ferrari's strength). British teams boycotted the 1960 race, citing safety reasons.

When circuits like Reims and the original Spa were dropped or tamed, so Monza became the acknowledged 'fastest race on the calendar', perfect for slipstreaming. In 1971 slipstreaming produced the closest finish of all time with cars using the slipstream down the final straight to pull alongside the leader at the flag. In 1971, five cars averaging 150 mph were separated at the line by

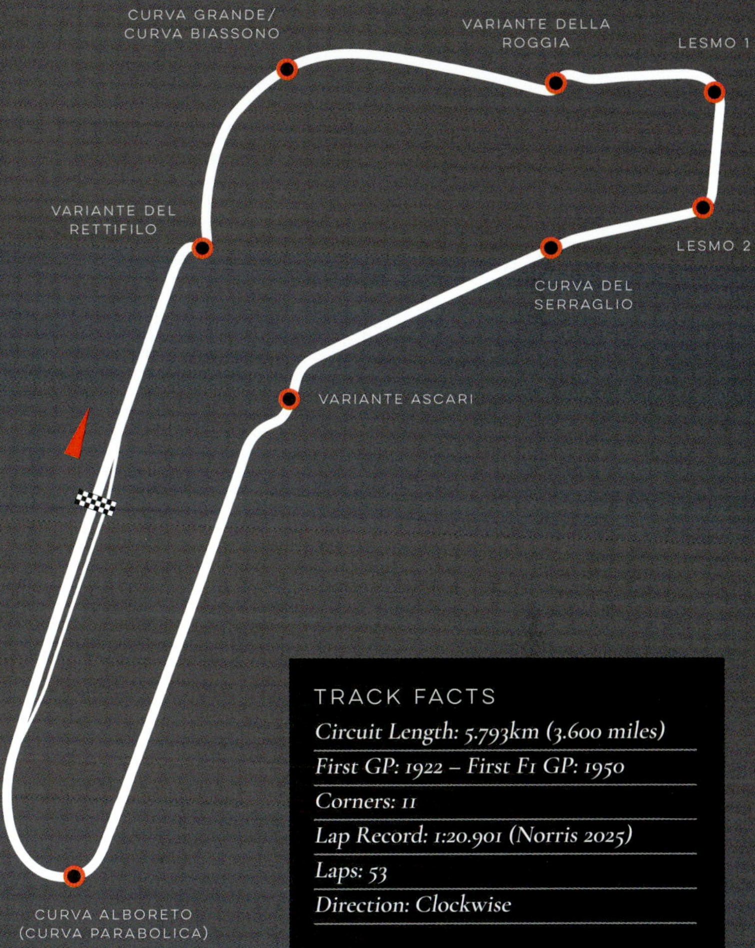

TRACK FACTS

Circuit Length: 5.793km (3.600 miles)

First GP: 1922 – First F1 GP: 1950

Corners: 11

Lap Record: 1:20.901 (Norris 2025)

Laps: 53

Direction: Clockwise

TOP: The best overtaking opportunity at Monza, the Variante del Rettifilo.
ABOVE: Looking down the main straight at Monza with the first chicane at bottom, 180-degree Parabolica at top, and the old Oval banking curving to the bottom left corner.

0.61 of a second. Peter Gethin in a BRM edged ahead of Ronnie Peterson's March by 0.1 seconds.

Chicanes were added to slow the cars on track at the Variante del Rettifilo (first), the Variante della Roggia (second) and after the two Lesmo corners, the Ascari chicane, named after the Italian Ferrari driver. Alberto Ascari was killed there while informally testing a sports car, just days after he had driven into Monaco harbour during the 1955 grand prix.

With few corners and the longest time on full throttle – between 80-84% – Monza is still a test of engine power combined with a low-drag set-up.

NOTABLE RACES

1960: Phil Hill (Ferrari) becomes the first American to win an F1 GP, using the combined oval/road course.

1970: Jochen Rindt's Lotus ploughs into the barriers at Parabolica killing the Austrian, ultimately making him F1's only posthumous world champion.

1988: Williams' Jean Louis Schlesser ruins McLaren's perfect winning season by driving into the side of Ayrton Senna while being lapped.

2007: Sebastian Vettel scores a shock victory for Toro Rosso, the former Minardi team.

2022: Driving the Red Bull RB19 Max Verstappen scores his tenth win a row – a new F1 record.

AUSTIN

Formula 1 struggled for years to find a circuit worthy of the United States Grand Prix but found it in Austin. The Circuit of the Americas had a rocky financial start, rescued by promoter Bobby Epstein, who incorporated a lot of the elements of a grand prix weekend now mandated by Liberty Media. The teams love the Hermann Tilke-designed circuit, which incorporates gradients and many of the corner profiles of famous F1 tracks – Silverstone, Istanbulring and Hockenheim – along with one of the most memorable climbs to turn one.

TRACK FACTS

Circuit Length: 5.513km (3.426 miles)

First GP: 2012

Corners: 20

Lap Record: 1:36.169 (Leclerc 2019)

Laps: 56

Direction: Anti-Clockwise

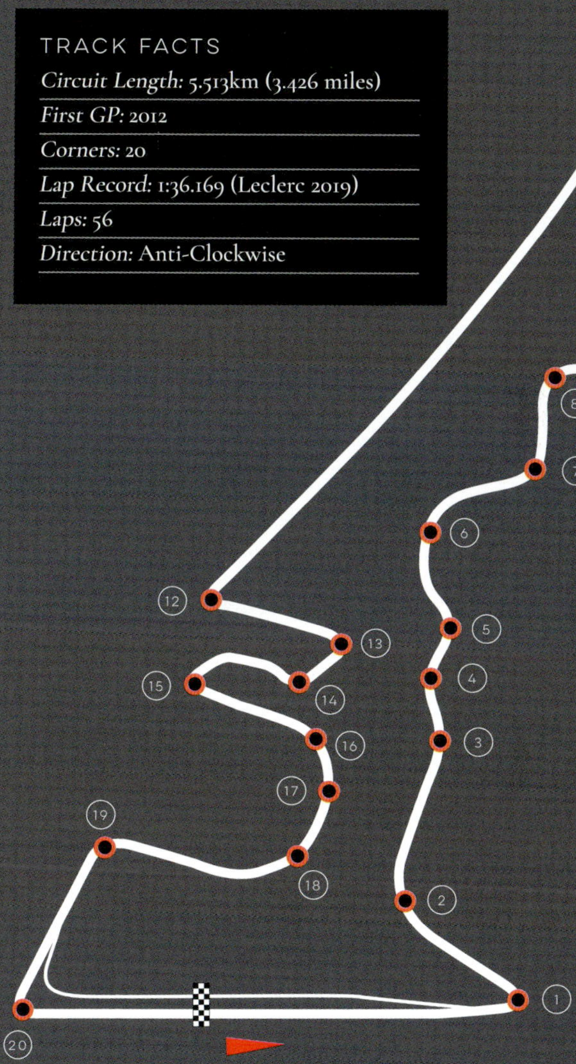

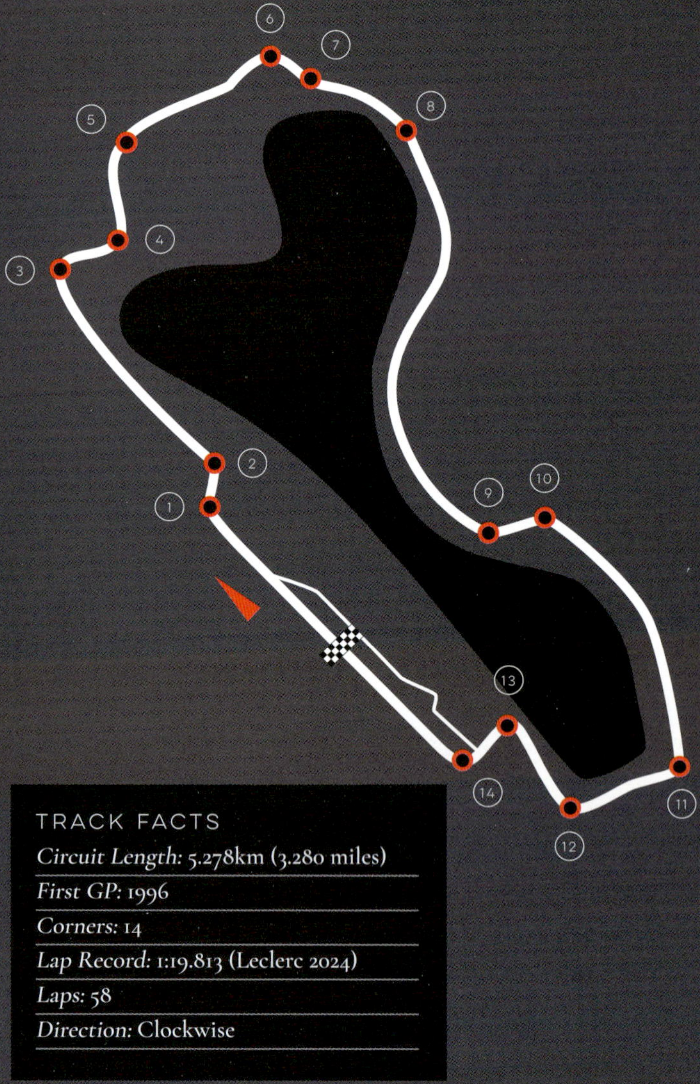

TRACK FACTS

Circuit Length: 5.278km (3.280 miles)

First GP: 1996

Corners: 14

Lap Record: 1:19.813 (Leclerc 2024)

Laps: 58

Direction: Clockwise

MELBOURNE

The Albert Park track is the traditional curtain-raiser for the F1 season, and it was here that teams finally realized that the 2020 season was postponed after the Covid outbreak. It's an atypical circuit in terms of car performance. Great pace in Melbourne doesn't necessarily translate to other tracks. No Australian driver has ever won their home race, so there is added pressure on Melbourne's Oscar Piastri to delight the fans – in 2025 a record 465,000 turned up over the GP weekend, proving to any local doubters that it was a financial asset for the city.

SUZUKA

Often described as 'Old School', the Honda-owned circuit has been used since 1987, more recent than the Hungaroring. The limited run-offs at Degner 1 and 2 (named after an East German motorcyclist who crashed there) belong to the past but they are an accepted challenge on F1's only figure-of-eight track. The once fearsome 130R corner has been neutered in recent years, but the S-Curves following turns one and two present F1 drivers with some fast switchbacks in which an F1 car comes alive.

TRACK FACTS

Circuit Length: 5.807km (3.608 miles)

First GP: 1987

Corners: 18

Lap Record: 1:30.965 (Antonelli 2025)

Laps: 53

Direction: Clockwise

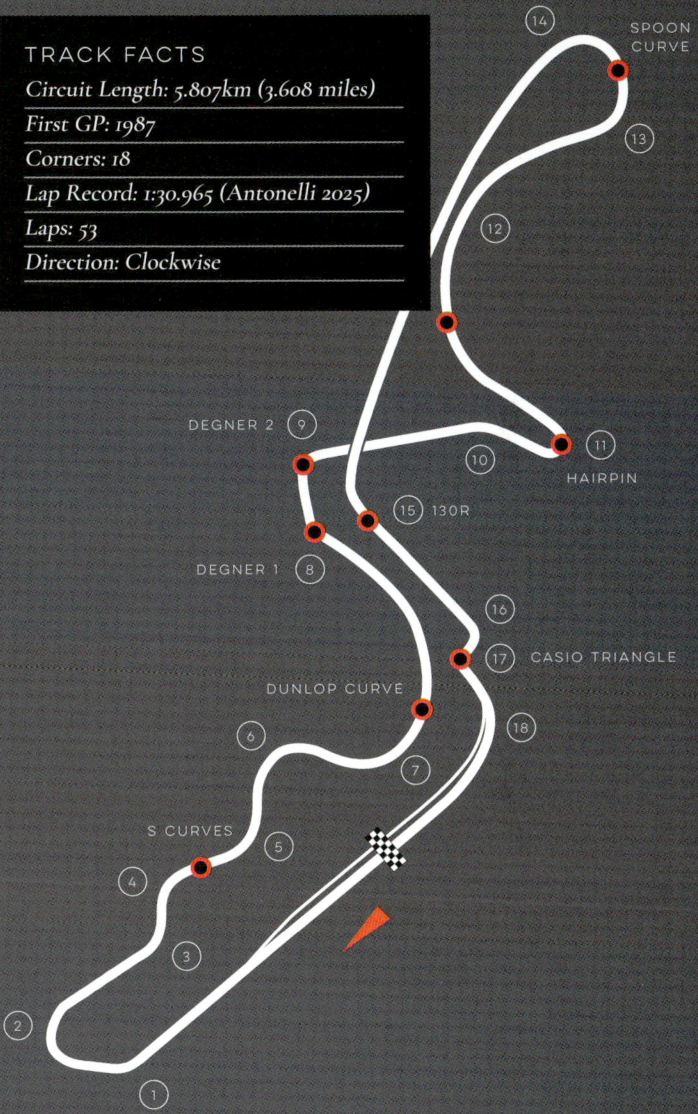

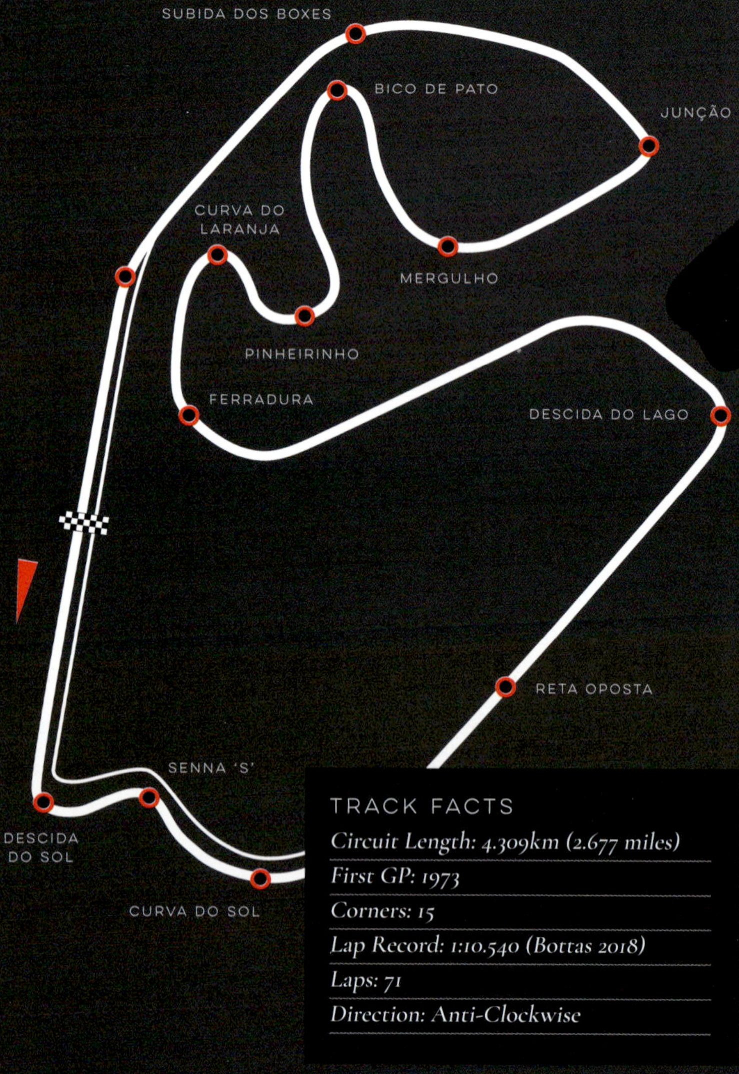

TRACK FACTS

Circuit Length: 4.309km (2.677 miles)

First GP: 1973

Corners: 15

Lap Record: 1:10.540 (Bottas 2018)

Laps: 71

Direction: Anti-Clockwise

INTERLAGOS

The Autódromo José Carlos Pace in São Paulo has seen many F1 showdowns. Before the arrival of the Abu Dhabi GP it was often the final race of the season and witnessed chaotic climaxes in 2008 and 2012. Originally it was almost double the size, running beyond the lake at *Descido do Lago* and looping back on itself, but in 1990 it was cut in half to 4.3 km. Ayrton Senna finally won his home race here in 1991, while local boy Rubens Barrichello never did in 19 attempts. The passionate Brazilian fans make this a stand-out race for locals, but visitors need to be wary about security.

BAHRAIN

The Bahrain Grand Prix made its debut in 2004, the first Middle-Eastern circuit and a trend-setter. In 2014, the rocky barren outcrops disappeared as it became a night race. It will stay on the F1 race calendar till 2036.

TRACK FACTS

Circuit Length: 5.412km (3.363 miles)

First GP: 2004

Corners: 15

Lap Record: 1:31.447 (de la Rosa 2005)

Laps: 58

Direction: Clockwise

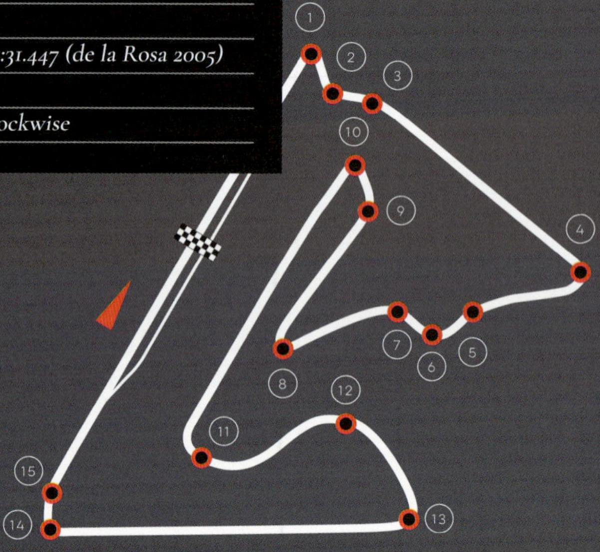

SHANGHAI

Shaped to resemble the Chinese character 'shang', Hermann Tilke' s circuit includes the incredibly tight turns 1, 2 and 3 where the outside line at the start of the race can often pay dividends.

TRACK FACTS

Circuit Length: 5.451km (3.387 miles)

First GP: 2004

Corners: 16

Lap Record: 1:32.238 (Schumacher 2004)

Laps: 56

Direction: Clockwise

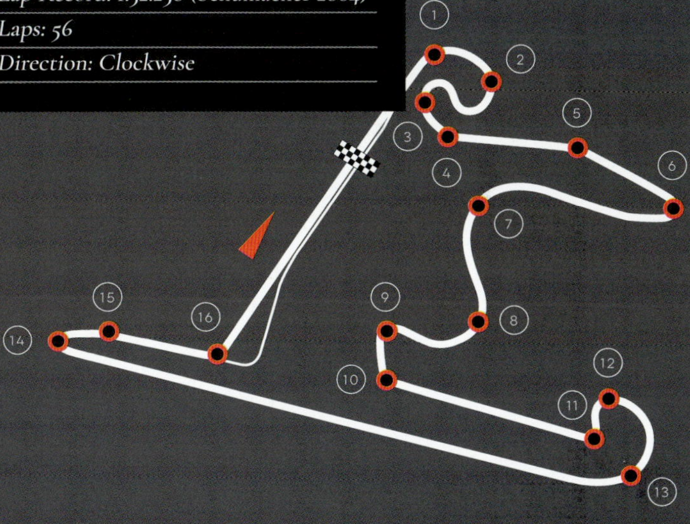

RED BULL RING

The old Österreichring was a flat-out blast which was shortened to the wider and more muted A1-Ring. With heavy investment from Red Bull it returned as the Red Bull Ring, beloved of Max Verstappen's Oranj Army.

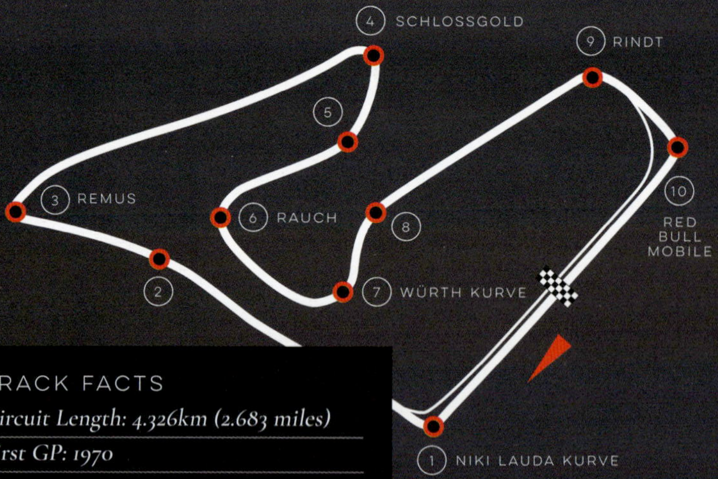

TRACK FACTS

Circuit Length: 4.326km (2.683 miles)

First GP: 1970

Corners: 10

Lap Record: 1:07.924 (Piastri 2025)

Laps: 71

Direction: Clockwise

BAKU

Oil money funded Azerbaijan's bid to be put on the world sporting map. The Baku street track has the narrowest strip of circuit through the castle section and it is a race that often provides controversy and drama.

TRACK FACTS

Circuit Length: 6.003km (3.730 miles)

First GP: 2016

Corners: 20

Lap Record: 1:43.009 (Leclerc 2019)

Laps: 51

Direction: Anti-Clockwise

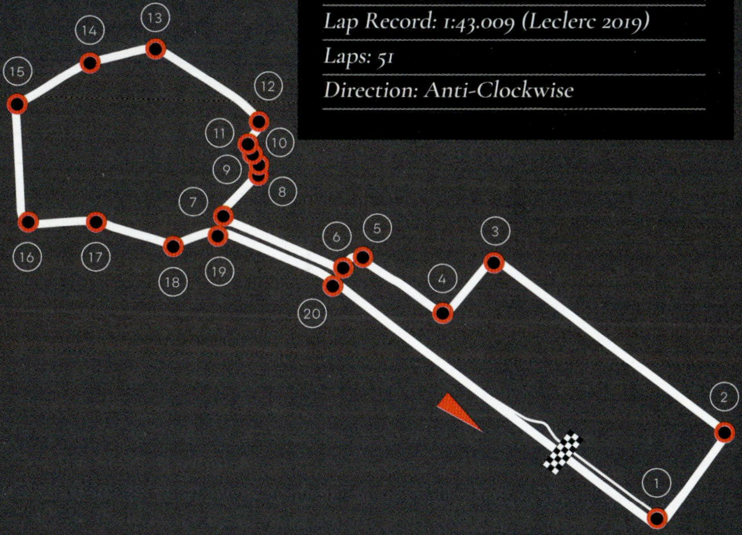

MONTREAL

First raced in 1978 when local hero Gilles Villeneuve took his debut GP win for Ferrari, the Île Notre Dame circuit was built on the site of Montreal's Expo 67 site, an island in the St. Lawrence River.

TRACK FACTS

Circuit Length: 4.361km (2.710 miles)

First GP: 1978

Corners: 14

Lap Record: 1:13.078 (Bottas 2019)

Laps: 70

Direction: Clockwise

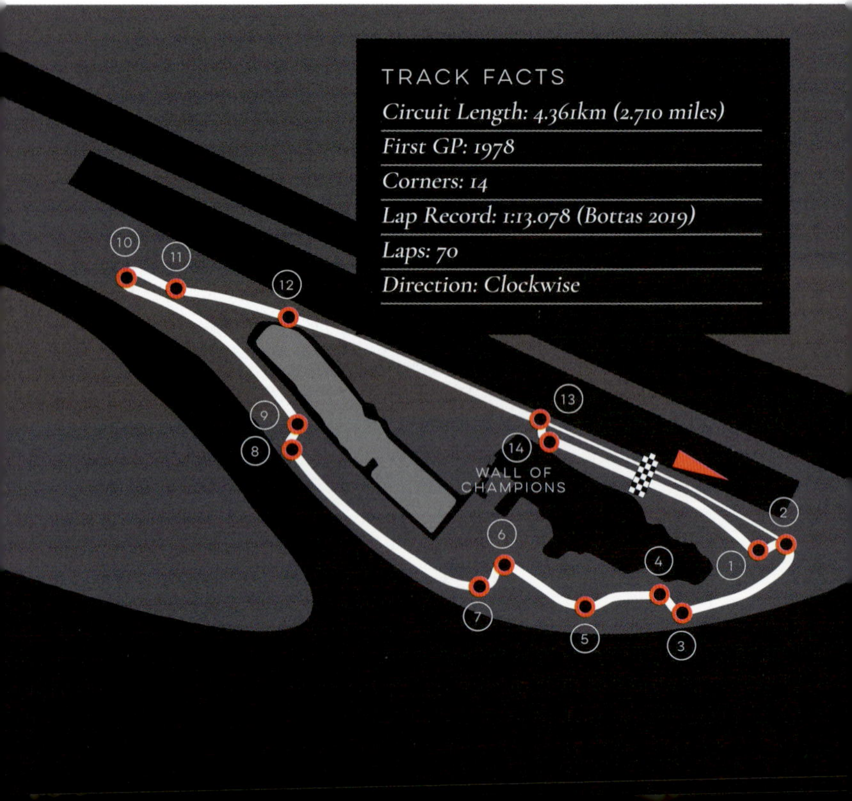

MIAMI

One of F1's most recent additions, the street track that circles the Hard Rock Stadium has become an instant favourite. Located 16 miles north of downtown Miami, the circuit has its own trackside faux yacht marina.

TRACK FACTS

Circuit Length: 5.412km (3.363 miles)

First GP: 2022

Corners: 19

Lap Record: 1:29.708 (Verstappen 2023)

Laps: 57

Direction: Anti-Clockwise

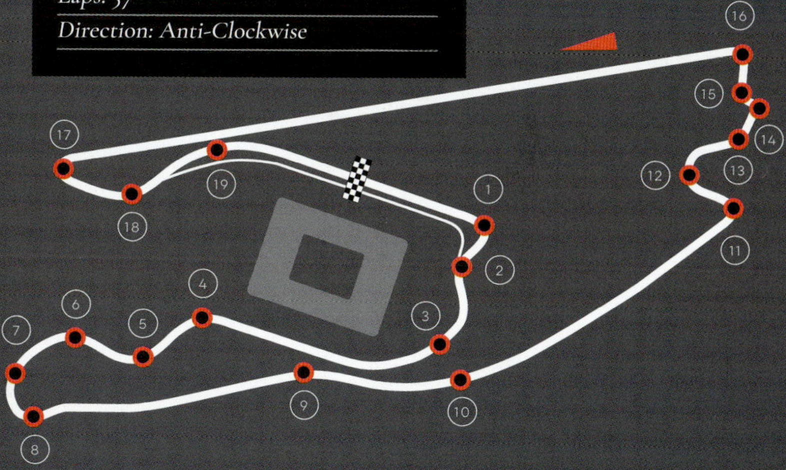

SINGAPORE

The pioneer of night racing in 2008, Singapore withstood the scandal of 'Crashgate' to put night races on the map. The Marina Bay circuit features many of the landmarks of old Singapore including the Anderson Bridge.

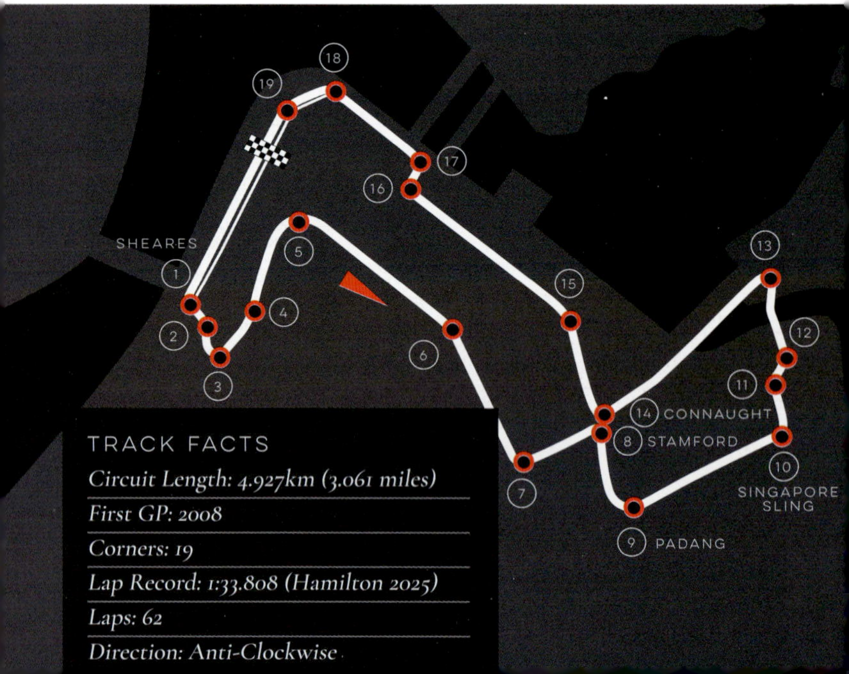

TRACK FACTS

Circuit Length: 4.927km (3.061 miles)

First GP: 2008

Corners: 19

Lap Record: 1:33.808 (Hamilton 2025)

Laps: 62

Direction: Anti-Clockwise

ABU DHABI

The circuit at Yas Marina hosted F1's first day-night race in 2009, The Abu Dhabi GP promoters pay Formula One Management extra to host the prestigious final race on the calendar, a position it will hold until at least 2030.

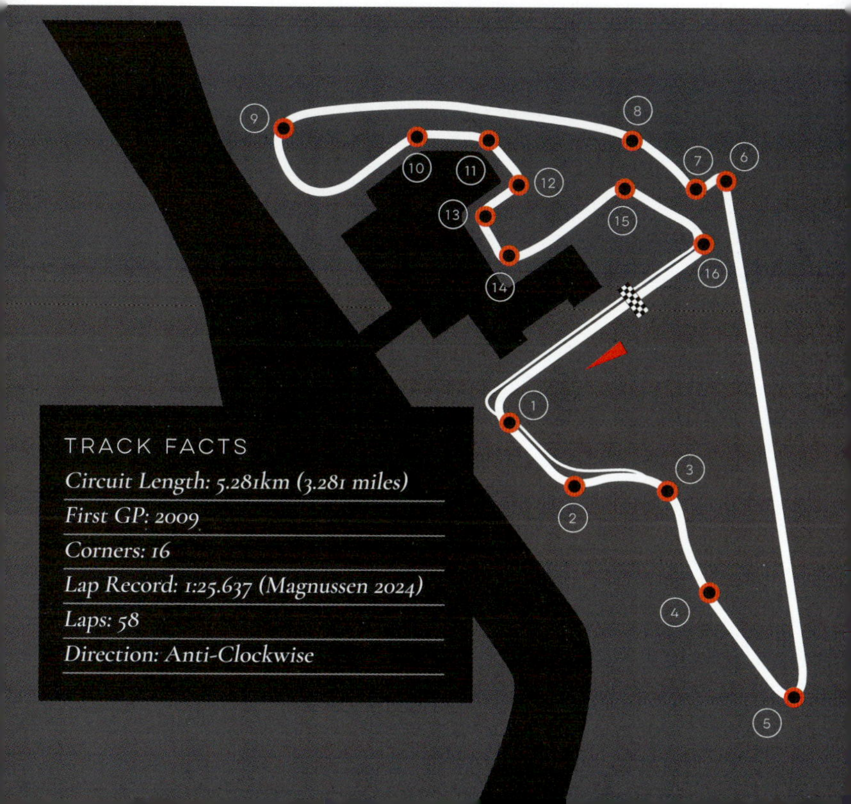

TRACK FACTS

Circuit Length: 5.281km (3.281 miles)

First GP: 2009

Corners: 16

Lap Record: 1:25.637 (Magnussen 2024)

Laps: 58

Direction: Anti-Clockwise

CISCO

F1 HEROES

ENZO FERRARI

Born in Modena in February 1898, Enzo Ferrari began his career as a driver. In 1924 he won the first Coppa Acerbo, racing along the dusty hillside roads above Pescara in an Alfa Romeo. He founded Scuderia Ferrari in 1929, running Alfa Romeos, and later took on the role of managing Alfa's official team.

From 1947, Enzo began to manufacture cars under his own name. Alberto Ascari took the Ferrari 125 F1 to second place in the 1950 Monaco GP, Ferrari's first Formula 1 start. A year later it was the 'Pampas Bull' Froilan Gonzalez behind the wheel of the Ferrari 375 who took the team's first win at Silverstone. Ferrari would win three grands prix that year to Alfa Romeo's four and when Alfa pulled out at the end of the year, Ferrari swept the board in 1952 with its 500 car, driven by Alberto Ascari.

In the 1950s Ferrari gained a reputation for pushing his drivers. Eugene Castelotti died while testing a car and *Il Commendatore* appeared more concerned about losing the car. Peter Collins and Luigi Musso both died behind the wheels of a Ferrari, but there was a national outcry when Spanish nobleman Alfonso de Portago was killed after a tyre blow-out in his Ferrari sportscar in the 1957 Mille Miglia, an accident that killed nine spectators, including five children.

PREVIOUS PAGE: Lando Norris is hoisted aloft by his mechanics after winning the Miami GP.
ABOVE: *Il Commendatore* at the wheel of one of his beloved sportscars.

A truculent and enigmatic figure, Enzo Ferrari rarely left Italy, or even Maranello, home to the Ferrari factory, and managed to weather the storm of impudent 'garagistes' from Britain in their nimble, rear-engined cars that helped inspire the classic 'sharknose' Ferrari 156 of 1961.

He oversaw world championships for Phil Hill and John Surtees in 1961 and 1964 before the Climax and Cosworth engines dominated the rest of the 1960s. Niki Lauda returned the marque to winning ways in 1975 and 1977, but the 'Old Man' couldn't hide his frustration at Lauda pulling out of the 1976 title-deciding Japanese GP, despite Niki's heroic return to the grid that year, six weeks after being given the last rites.

His sportscars may have dominated the Le Mans 24 Hours race, but after the 1979 driver's title for Jody Scheckter, the next would not arrive till the following century. Seemingly aloof, he was genuinely affected by the loss of 'favourite son' Gilles Villeneuve in a needless 1982 practice accident at Zolder. When Enzo Ferrari died, aged 90 in 1988, the nation mourned and Gerhard Berger and Michele Alboreto finished first and second for the team at Monza, in a year when the dominant McLaren looked like winning every race.

LEFT: Enzo Ferrari in conversation with sportscar designer Battista Pininfarina in 1964.

ABOVE: Fangio's record is unique; no other driver has won titles with four different teams.

JUAN MANUEL FANGIO

An Argentine of Italian descent, Juan Manuel Fangio honed his driving – and survival – skills on long road races in South America, such as the 1940 Gran Premio del Norte, which was 10,000 km (6,250 miles) long. It ran from Buenos Aires up through the high Andes to Bolivia and Peru, and then back to Buenos Aires, taking 15 days. Winning the race gained the former car mechanic national acclaim.

When he moved to Europe he raced Alfa Romeos and in 1950 matched 'Nino' Farina's three F1 wins, but failed to take the title. At 40 years old he became world champion for Alfa in 1951, was sidelined with a broken neck in 1952, and came up against Alberto Ascari in a dominant Ferrari 500 in 1953.

He then reeled off another four titles won with an unprecedented three different manufacturers: Mercedes-Benz (1954-1955), Ferrari (1956) and Maserati (1957). His most remarkable achievement was in his final race, pulling back 51 seconds in the last 10 laps of the German Grand Prix at the old Nürburgring, overhauling two Ferraris to win the championship for Maserati at the grand old age of 46.

COLIN CHAPMAN

Colin Chapman designed the championship-winning Vanwall of 1958, but is best remembered for relentless F1 innovation with his Lotus team. Chapman had a reputation for building fast-but-fragile, lightweight cars, such as the Lotus 25, 33 and 49.

In 1962, the Lotus 25 featured F1's first fully stressed monocoque chassis. Driven by Jim Clark it took drivers' and constructors' titles in 1963, while the Lotus 33 took both in 1965. Equipped with a Cosworth engine, the Lotus 49 took the title with Graham Hill at the wheel in 1968 after Clark's untimely demise in an F2 race at Hockenheim.

Chapman then set about adapting some of the techniques employed by Jim Hall on his Chaparral sportscars. First came the ungainly skyscraper wings which were prone to failure. Banned from 1969, these were followed by lower rear wings on the Lotus 72 which featured a pioneering wedge shape. It took world titles in 1970 and 1972. Another Hall innovation was 'ground effect' cars, where the underside of the chassis was turned into a Venturi tunnel with flexible side skirts that 'sucked' the car to the road. Mario Andretti took the Lotus 78 to his sole world title in 1978, Chapman's final fling before his death in 1982.

RIGHT: Chapman (left) in the pits with Lotus driver Jim Clark in 1965.

ATION
SER

NIKI LAUDA

Niki Lauda's wealthy Viennese family didn't approve of his sporting ambition. His grandfather, a bank board member, prevented his grandson getting the loan he needed to buy a full-time F1 seat with March in 1972. Resourceful as ever, Lauda went to a rival Austrian bank who were delighted to have their logo on Lauda's helmet.

His March season was a disappointment, Niki describing the car in typically blunt terms. He then bluffed his way into a BRM drive for 1973 with sponsorship he didn't possess, and was relieved when boss Louis Stanley offered him the drive for nothing. Ferrari had also spotted his genius and levered him into a seat with the Scuderia for 1974. Driving the iconic Ferrari 312T he was world champion in 1975, survived the fiery inferno of his Nürgburgring crash in 1976 – when he was rescued by his fellow drivers – and only failed to win the championship in the final race at Mount Fuji. His astonishing return is one of F1's most courageous stories, yet he was unsupported by Enzo Ferrari and after winning again in 1977 quit the team before season end.

A short retirement was followed by a comeback with McLaren and a world championship snatched by half a point from Alain Prost in 1984, after which he became a trusted advisor to the Mercedes team.

AYRTON SENNA

Ayrton Senna da Silva is regarded by many as the greatest F1 driver of all time. The Brazilian's incredible recall of a practice lap made him an engineer's dream, long before telemetry provided all the information. He was aggressive on track and dominated in junior single-seaters, battling hard with Martin Brundle for the British F3 championship in 1983. His debut season in the underpowered Toleman-Hart could have brought a shock victory in the rain at Monaco – starting 13th, he was rapidly catching Alain Prost's McLaren, when the Frenchman's frantic signalling to the Clerk of the Course got the grand prix red-flagged.

Moving up to Lotus, he scored a debut win at Estoril in 1985 but his major break was signing for McLaren in 1988. Senna joined double world champion Alain Prost in the most acrimonious driver pairing the sport had witnessed. The McLaren-Honda M4/4 was unbeatable that season, winning 15 of 16 races and with eight victories Ayrton took his first drivers' title, eclipsing Prost. Their rivalry culminated in Prost deliberately driving into Senna before the chicane at Suzuka in the penultimate race. Prost exited his car, but Senna got a legitimate push-start from the marshals, pitted for a new front wing and drove to a storming victory.

BOSS
MEN'S FASHION
BOSS
MEN'S FASHION

NACIONAL
elf

French president of the FIA, Jean-Marie Balestre intervened and Senna was disqualified for cutting the chicane. Prost then took the resulting world champion's No.1 to Ferrari for 1990. At season end, when they lined up at Suzuka, Senna led Prost in the championship and returned the favour, cynically taking the Frenchman out at turn one to claim his second title. He won again in 1991 and partly confessed his deliberate move of the previous year.

With the loss of Honda engines McLaren struggled, so a move to the now-dominant Williams team in 1994 and an Adrian Newey-designed car seemed like world title No.4 would be a formality. Except F1 had removed all the technical gizmos, such as active and reactive suspension, partly thanks to an intervention by Senna himself. Designers Patrick Head and Newey had miscalculated the effects brought on by a reduced window for adjusting ride height in their new car. At Imola, when his Williams FW16 hit a bump after the fast Tamburello corner, Senna's car snapped sideways, hit the barriers and a suspension arm was bent backwards into his helmet in what otherwise could have been a survivable accident. Brazil and F1 went into shock, having suddenly lost its greatest talent.

TOP LEFT: Ayrton Senna and Alain Prost approach Copse corner at the 1989 British GP.
LEFT: Senna debriefs engineer Alan Brown in the Interlagos pits, 1994.

MICHAEL SCHUMACHER

Michael Schumacher's father owned a kart circuit near Kerpen and so 'Schumi' was able to develop his skills from a young age. He became part of the Mercedes World Sportscar team along with Heinz-Harald Frentzen, considered the driver most likely to reach F1. Except a surprise vacancy in the Jordan team at the 1991 Belgian GP gave him the opportunity for a one-off drive. Michael qualified seventh, four places in front of his more experienced team-mate, and the next race he was a Benetton driver.

Back-to-back world titles in 1994 and 1995 were clouded by allegations the team were using banned traction control, along with Schumacher's questionable crash with Damon Hill in Adelaide at the title-deciding race. However, his superb mastery of wet conditions and a single-minded determination to push the Ferrari team forward from 1996 eventually brought him five championships in a row between 2000 and 2004 – titles masterminded by Ross Brawn and Jean Todt, who made it quite clear that Michael was the No.1 driver. Following retirement and an unsuccessful return with Mercedes, it is ironic that Schumacher became a casualty of the sport he loved (skiing) as opposed to the dangerous sport in which he excelled.

vodafone
Marlboro
vodafone
L'ORÉAL
PARIS

cognizant
aramco
ASTON MARTIN
cognizant
FORMULA ONE™ TEAM
PERONI
cognizant
aramco

FERNANDO ALONSO

The much-travelled driver from Asturias in Northern Spain has had many teams in his 400-plus grand prix starts. Minardi, Renault, McLaren, Renault, Ferrari, McLaren, Alpine and finally Aston Martin have all been part of the journey.

Driving for Renault, Fernando beat McLaren's Kimi Räikkönen to the world title in 2005 and edged out Michael Schumacher for his second in 2006. However, his first year at McLaren in 2007 was filled with controversy along with the mistaken belief that he had signed as a No.1 driver with all the priority that entailed. At the end of the year he quit to return to his old boss Flavio Briatore. He was on the brink of two more titles with Ferrari in 2010 and 2012, but lost out in the final race of each season.

Rated by many as the equal in talent to Hamilton and Verstappen, Fernando's story is one of picking the wrong team at the wrong time. A planned move to Red Bull never came through and Alonso's return to McLaren coincided with the debut of an underpowered Honda engine, which he mocked. Things got so bad he took a sabbatical. His return to the grid with Alpine, at age 40, and then Aston Martin, showed that he had lost none of his edge in his relentless pursuit of another title.

LEWIS HAMILTON

Lewis Hamilton was a karting prodigy, at 10 the youngest winner of the national Cadet karting class, which handily brought him into contact with Ron Dennis at the 1995 Autosport Awards dinner. He famously approached the McLaren boss and told him he wanted to drive for his team and become world champion. Thirteen years later and he was back at the awards ceremony, mission accomplished.

McLaren had fast-tracked Hamilton into the team in 2007 in a fractious season rocked by sporting espionage, partnered with an abrasive Fernando Alonso, who thought he would be given No.1 status. Lewis came up short in Interlagos, but a year later he won the title in Brazil, passing Timo Glock for the 5th place he needed at the last corner, on the last lap, of the last race – and after rival Felipe Massa's family had begun celebrating.

The F1 paddock thought he was crazy to transfer to the unproven Mercedes team in 2013, but after winning a further six titles courtesy of the Silver Arrows' dominant hybrid engine it was a different narrative. His record-breaking eighth championship in 2021 slipped by thanks to an FIA race director failing to apply the rules. A 2025 move to Ferrari shocked F1 yet again, but adjusting to a new team (with no 'Bono' as engineer) proved a nightmare at first.

sparco
CASTORE
TAG HEUER
Mobil 1
VISA
AT&T
ROKT
RAUCH
Red Bull
Red Bull
MAX
Heineken
Red Bull

MAX VERSTAPPEN

Son of F1 driver Jos Verstappen and former karting champion Sophie Kumpen, Max Verstappen had both the genes and the hard taskmaster dad to push him through his karting apprenticeship. Halfway through his first single-seater series, Euro F3, aged just sixteen, he signed for Red Bull. He chose the Austrian team over Mercedes because they offered him a race seat for 2015. He took part in first practice for Toro Rosso at the 2014 Japanese GP aged 17 years and three days, the youngest driver to participate in an F1 weekend.

In his first season with Toro Rosso he was evenly matched with the more experienced Carlos Sainz. But in 2016, after disastrous early results for Daniil Kvyat (and pressure from Jos), Max took his seat alongside Daniel Ricciardo at Red Bull ... and then won his very first race, the 2016 Spanish GP, re-setting many 'Youngest in F1' records. Though Ricciardo outscored him over two seasons, reaction to their clash in Baku told him that Max was the favoured son and he left for Renault.

Max continued to hone his skills with a naturally aggressive style in Adrian Newey's increasingly competitive chassis. In 2021 Max was able to wrest the driver's title from Lewis Hamilton in a dramatic season of twists and turns. Three titles followed from 2022 to 2024.

LANDO NORRIS

A well-funded Lando Norris catapulted through the ranks of European karting, rubbing shoulders with the likes of Max Verstappen, Charles Leclerc and Pierre Gasly. He was picked up by the McLaren Driver Development Programme in 2017 and Zak Brown partnered him with Carlos Sainz for his rookie F1 season in 2019. Lando outqualified the more experienced Spaniard 11-10 that year.

His first podium came in 2020 at the Austrian GP, making him the third youngest podium-finisher in F1 at the time. He took his maiden pole position in changeable conditions at the 2021 Russian GP in Sochi and a win looked likely until the McLaren team botched his late-race strategy. The debut win proved elusive, however, and at the start of the 2023 season it looked further away than ever. But a dramatic turnaround mid season saw them back in contention. In 2023 Norris had qualified 16th at the Miami GP. A year later he won the race and with Max Verstappen's results falling off there was almost the prospect of a title challenge. That arrived in 2025 when for most of the season he battled team-mate Oscar Piastri under McLaren's 'papaya rules'. Scrupulous fairness opened the door for a resurgent Verstappen, but carefully executed McLaren strategy at the final race allowed Norris to clinch his first world title by just two points.

avenga
CASTORE

PICTURE CREDITS

The publishers would like to thank the following for permission to reproduce copyright material. All reasonable efforts have been made to trace copyright holders and to obtain their permission for the use of copyright material. The publishers apologize for any errors or omissions and will gratefully incorporate any corrections in future reprints if notified.

t: top, b: bottom, l: left, r: right

FIA: 47

FOM: 96b

Getty Images: 6 Alastair Staley ; 13 Klementaski Collection; 28 Joe Portlock; 30, 67b Rudy Carezzevoli; 39 Mark Thompson; 43t, 80 Andrej Isakovic; 44 Clive Rose; 48t NurPhoto; 48b Mark Sutton; 50 Peter Fox; 117 Racing One; 120 Keystone-France.

Grand Prix Photo.com/Peter Nygaard: Front cover and 8, 10, 14,17, 18, 21, 22, 25, 26, 33, 35, 36, 40, 43b, 52, 55, 56, 59, 60, 63, 64, 67t, 68, 70, 73, 75, 76, 85, 88, 92, 96t, 98, 101, 102, 105, 114, 118, 123, 124, 127, 128, 131, 132, 135, 136,139.

Circuit illustrations by Cara Rogers

AUTHOR ACKNOWLEDGEMENTS

The author would like to thank the indefatigable Peter Nygaard, whose photos form the core of this book. He has been attending F1 races as a journalist and photographer since the late 1970s and his capacity to absorb the rigours and vagaries of a 20-plus race schedule across the globe each year and still stay cheerful is remarkable.

OTHER BOOKS AVAILABLE

ISBN: 978-1-78840-698-7

ISBN: 978-1-78840-697-0

RAISING READERS
Books Build Bright Futures

Dear Reader,

We'd love your attention for one more page to tell you about the crisis in children's reading, and what we can all do.

Studies have shown that reading for fun is the **single biggest predictor of a child's future life chances** – more than family circumstance, parents' educational background or income. It improves academic results, mental health, wealth, communication skills, ambition and happiness.[1]

The number of children reading for fun is in rapid decline. Young people have a lot of competition for their time. In 2024, 1 in 10 children and young people in the UK aged 5 to 18 did not own a single book at home.[2]

Hachette works extensively with schools, libraries and literacy charities, but here are some ways we can all raise more readers:

- Reading to children for just 10 minutes a day makes a difference
- Don't give up if children aren't regular readers – there will be books for them!
- Visit bookshops and libraries to get recommendations
- Encourage them to listen to audiobooks
- Support school libraries
- Give books as gifts

There's a lot more information about how to encourage children to read on our website: **www.RaisingReaders.co.uk**

Thank you for reading.

hachette
LIVRE

[1] OECD, '21st-Century Readers: Developing Literacy Skills in a Digital World', 2021, https://www.oecd.org/en/publications/21st-century-readers_a83d84cb-en.html

[2] National Literacy Trust, 'Book Ownership in 2024'. November 2024, https://literacytrust.org.uk/research-services/research-reports/book-ownership-in-2024